INSCAPES
OF THE
CHILD'S WORLD

*Jungian Counseling
in Schools and Clinics*

JOHN ALLAN

Spring Publications, Inc.
Dallas, Texas

Published by Spring Publications, Inc.;
P.O. Box 222069; Dallas, Texas 75222
Printed in the United States of America
Text printed on acidfree paper
Cover designed and produced by Bharati Bhatia

Distributed in the United States by the Continuum Publishing
Group; in Canada by Maxwell Macmillan; in the United
Kingdom, Eire, and Europe by Airlift Book Co.; in Australia
by Astam Books Pty Ltd; in Europe by Daimon Verlag

Library of Congress Cataloging-in-Publication Data

Allan, John A. B. (John Alexander Bonnell), 1941–
    Inscapes of the child's world.

Bibliography: p.
1. Child psychotherapy.   2. Children—Counseling of.
3. Jung, C. G. (Carl Gustav), 1875–1961.   I. Title.
RJ504.A43 1988   618.92'891'14   88–27831
            ISBN 0–88214–338–7 (pbk.)

Inscapes
of the
Child's World

For my father
John Balfour Allan
and
my teachers
Don Sampson and Thomas Parker
with gratitude

"Dawn is born at midnight."

C. G. JUNG

Contents

List of Figures

Foreword

THOUGH YOU AND I once were children and may now be parents, and may even be dedicating our working lives to the care and counseling of children, we hardly know them. What really is a child, this state called childhood, or adolescence, and who is this particular child now in my charge? Why do children seem a people apart—as we say "men, women, and children"? Why so fascinating, enraging, wondrous, and incomprehensible?

The smaller the child, the more this is the case. The Platonists, and the Romantics who followed them, had a theory to account for our feelings of the child's strangeness, its peculiar terrors and pleasures. The child's soul descends, they said, from another archetypal world, entering this world trailing clouds of glory as it comes (Wordsworth). A being close to angels, it arrives knowing everything essential. Or, as we would say: its collective unconscious is replete with primordial awareness. This angelic guise was demonstrated by pointing at the child's skin when a baby, its face when asleep, its smile, its startling inventive freedom. The angelic guise became a standard icon in graveyard stone and nursery-book lithograph during the last century especially. Only in this century of our Western history has the child been overburdened with carrying the "bad seed" of our civilization's disorder. Today, children everywhere are worried about and need "help," from infant massage to play therapy to corrective lessons. Something is always "wrong" with them.

The soul's difficulties with its descent into the world show up in counseling as "adjustment disorders" or, worse, as autism, mutism, attention deficit, anti-social behavior, and the other ills catalogued in our textbooks of abnormal psychology. From the Romantic perspective, the counselor serves as a midwife to the psyche—a role Socrates imagined for his work, guiding the child into the world without too much loss of its remnants of mythic memory. Or, to use another simile from classical Greece, the counselor is like a *paedogogos*, a slave or servant who walks along with a child to school.

School tries to put the child's psyche within the mind of practical reason: clocktime, factual truth, and a xerox notion of images, i.e., accurate reproduction. What you draw is what you see. School defines "realism" as photographic realism and tests the child's sense of reality in the hard schoolyard of competition. Coping before hoping. Realism, however, ever since Plato and still in philosophy today, refers to realities of invisible forms that are innate and pattern the actual world. A classical realist would say the child brings reality with him or her, a reality which today we call fantasy.

The child's fantasy is still in thrall to the "thing of beauty [that] is a joy forever," as Keats said. As he also said, this beauty is truth. Or, let us say, according to the Romantic vision beauty is the interior truth potentially available to the child to keep it on course. Beauty is as much a guide as reason, discipline and psychological know-how. The child's need for beauty as guide suggests the arts take primary place in the teaching and counseling of children. After all, the arts at least refer to beauty and must keep it in mind; whereas psychology, education and social studies seem completely unconscious of its importance in moving the soul deeply, so that beauty has become the Great Repressed in the training of professional counselors. The arts take primary place for another reason. They bridge between the child's first world of imagination and the actual world into which it descends, thereby providing a hands-on way of healing the most fundamental cleavage in human existence.

The daily pressures of work make us forget that the child as symbol, and actual children too, always evokes the twin possibilities of terror and joy, extremes at the outer edges of the curve of normality. The child enters the world still open to emotional intensities beyond the usual. This confronts the therapist often with emotions long dormant, even extinct, in his or her own soul. Those who have most to do with children seem to have lost the feeling for the child's terror and fascination with terror and, even more, to have lost the child's extraordinary possibility for joy. Instead, we meet children with worried concern, therapeutic goodwill and professional smiles, but few laughs. We would bring the child under the normalizing shelter of the bell curve: nothing to extremes. Keats and Blake and Whitman, however, insist on the wildest joy.

Freud did too. He saw the child's sensuous delight in all things as a polymorphous sexual libido. The child enters the world packed with the pleasure principle, a roly-poly of desires for what the world offers. Like a goat's kid, the child dances with surplus exuberance; like a kitten it explores everywhere and takes sudden fright; and like a piglet, how good it all tastes! The world is a good place to be—when, and only when, the imagination with which the child descends is still alive enough to imbue the things of the world with the child's vision of beauty.

Not its innocence makes the child's psyche so susceptible to corruption of its desire, but its attachment to beauty. Eating disorders, media addiction, hyperactivity and victimization by exploiters are based in the child's native desire for beauty in this world comparable to the richness of its fantasy in the unconscious soul. Exploitation could not occur if a child entered the world a mere *tabula rasa* void of any prior delight in and recognition of sensate images. So, the disorders of sensationalism reveal the child's innate aesthetic response to the world as a place of pleasure, in which all things are desirable. *Schlaraffenland* and Paradise are where we begin, and the child will live in a cargo cult of consumerism when the fantasies of the extra-ordinary that fill its soul are not given imaginary and imaginative response by its adult guides.

But many adult guides who meet the disturbed child are themselves disturbed by their training. We have been initiated into the myth of developmental psychology: that all life moves in one direction starting in infancy (but not before, not beyond). Moreover, the simplistics of our myth say that this one-way direction in time is causal: a person is caused by history, and the earlier the history the more powerful the cause. So, childhood has been declared the source of all our disaffected behavior. This tale told by dynamic and developmental psychology says childhood is basically miserable. Every therapy session searches memory for traces of unhappiness. We do not turn there for beauty and joy, but to uncover the curses of abuse, shame, and fixation on that abuse and shame. Bad mothers, absent fathers and envious siblings are the demons and ogres in psychology's fairy tale. This script curses the family with a psychology of blame instead of honor. It also curses the pleasurable world and the origins of the libido in sensuous joy. No wonder that actual children become so anesthetized that they are content with the pseudo stimuli of TV, so that by adolescence they have to shoot up to feel. They sit in classes without motivation, walk the streets in sullen rage, and seek desperately for sensuous transcendence in sounds, speeds and sex for an altered state of mind as an alternative script to the soulless and joyless dealing, handling, coping, managing life as a program of practical reason. Unconsciously, they recollect something else, something more, which they would find again, sometimes by suicide.

To get some of this off my chest, or out of my heart, and to offer a *vision* of children, I welcomed John Allan's invitation to write a foreword to his book. As his colleague, his friend, and now his publisher, I am enthused by his book. It is important. He shows a way that is practical, sober and unassuming for the great escape from reasonable realism, backward and inward to the inscapes of the child's soul by restoring the authenticity of the child's own visionary activity. He gives detailed instructions for coaxing the child into its inscapes, into the forgotten terrain of its interior knowledge, the recovery of which is healing. He knows the children and their plight; he knows the imagination and its force; and he also knows the counselors, their encouraging tendencies and their possible wrong reactions. For, after all, the counselor is obliged to engage in a world of witches and wizards, of violent wars and drowning babies, of quicksand and pathetically withering flowers, a world from which his or her training has yielded little more than alienation. To engage in the child's fantasy requires one to be engaged by one's own. To enjoy one's own dreams and be comfortable in one's own inscapes should be the first requirement for working with children. This book makes this requirement a pleasure, for John Allan leads the reader into the forest, gently, and with the practical know-how of a naturalist.

The beauty of the book lies just there. It gives the reader the in-scape without heavy theoretical equipment, without psycho-dynamic bulldozing. It is a book without argument—for the imagination doesn't argue—a book without accusations against social forces, bad parents, the curse of poverty. Sure, all that is always present: ugly abuse, crass stupidity, misfortune. Yet, through it all we watch the actual display of each child's fantasy, telling its stories and painting its pictures as it slowly disengages from the mess in that process we call therapy. For me, the prime virtue of this book is its good sense. John Allan is not, like me, an intoxicated Romantic. Nor is he out to attest to the archetypes developing into the Jungian Self. He wishes to—and does—lay bare what actually happens with schoolchildren when their in-scapes are wisely received and allowed to form. If we must use that abused word "creative," then here is witness to its simply happen-ing. All the while the prose is straightforward, the information comprehensive, detailed, and instructive, packed into the pages, with little fuss. As Allan says in his Introduction, he wanted to be a forester. In this book he is taking care of the trees.

For a good example of his know-how, turn to chapter 8, the case of the five-and-a-half-year-old psychotic girl, Luci. She comes with a dream of having visited the "dead land"—"no people, no fires in the fireplaces, no food in the refrigerators, no beds in the bedrooms, and no furniture in the living rooms. Outside there are no flowers, no grass, only rocks." Luci's psyche is in the wasteland of a "deep depression," as Allan says. But notice, he does not jerk her out of it, console her with mothering, or fear for her dissolu-tion. The image tells him where she is, and he enters that place with her and speaks with her from within the inscape, trusting that a *vis naturalis* (a natural life force) is working its way within the psyche even in the "dead land" or mythical Underworld, in the shape of images and the colors of feelings.

Another hint we may gain from the book concerns interpreta-tion. When and how do we interpret a child's images? Allan sug-gests (chapter 2) that at certain moments the counselor make "linkages . . . from the drawings to the therapeutic relationship or to outer world situations." He gives this example:

I see the helicopter pilot is repairing the hole in the road. . . . I wonder if at times you feel I'm like that pilot helping you mend some of your hurts.

Here we watch the way interpretation acts as a bridge between worlds, teaching the practicality of metaphor for helping the descent from images into experiences. For the child here learns how one and the same image—helicopter pilot repairing holes, i.e., whirley-bird-man or sky hero performing the archetypal task of shoring up human culture—is at the same time concerned directly with the personal fate of the child himself. The holes are not in the child or made by the child. He is not they, any more than the pilot is he. Nor are the holes directly the result of past abuse any more than the pilot is the present representative of the helping therapist. These implications of the image are drawn from it by interpretation. The image itself, however, remains intact as the actual healing factor because it gives the child a way of picturing in metaphorical terms his drama, fostering his imagination to go on the road of his life and meet his plight by the innate means of "dreaming the myth onward," as Jung defined his therapeutic method.

Interpretation exercises our metaphorical thinking, that capacity to realize on several levels at once. We learn to grasp that the exotic world of symbolic scenes and the painful world of human relationships can be in continuing relation.

Despite Allan's advice regarding interpretation and the book's many demonstrations of it, he does maintain (chapter 5), in accord with the Jungian view, that imaginative expression in the presence of the counselor with no interpretation helps children release some of the power of symbols and their emotions at a critical moment in their lives. Again, we see his reliance upon the child's own psychic images, what Jung calls the symbolic process of individuation, a deep-rooted autonomous activity that strives like the energy in a tree or the instinctual vitality in any living form to maintain its integrity in face of its destiny—even if that destiny be early death due to illness or accident.

I would also point out that this integrity in the practice of counseling begins with the respect Allan shows for the integrity of the images themselves. If we reduce the images back to our assessment of the child's personality (his violent hostility or her mute fright) or to traumata suffered by the child from the environment, we are not recognizing the full authority of the images in shaping the child's destiny. We are not allowing what the child brings with him or her into the world, in the Platonic and Romantic sense of an innate capacity to form life in accordance with imagination (or, as Jung wrote, "fantasy creates reality every day"). Our task is to nurture the child by nurturing its inscapes.

For instance, Allan (chapter 5) emphasizes "talking about the content of the picture in the third person ('I notice you've drawn a big gorilla; I wondered what the gorilla is thinking . . . feeling . . . and planning to do next')."

Had Allan said—and here I am inventing a scenario—"I guess that gorilla reminds you of your father when he gets in that 'state' after drinking," or had said, "I guess that gorilla is how you feel when you tear up your room and want to beat up on your little brother," then the gorilla would have lost its potency as a living being of imagination and been reduced to a mere component of the rational world, explained as a function of personality (the child's rage) or a residue of experience (the child's terrifyingly drunken father image).

Instead, Allan invites the gorilla to step out of the drawing and speak. This gesture toward the image respects its autonomy. The gorilla becomes a partner in the counsel: child, counselor, and gorilla. The two persons turn directly to the personified image for understanding why it has appeared, what it feels, how it plans to move; thereby the child—and the counselor—can possibly foresee in which direction within the crisis of the child's destiny the next phase might go.

The invitation to the gorilla to speak is so radical that it moves counseling itself outside our culture into other times and places, and into another myth beyond humanism. In the Middle Ages, this turn to the image would be demonism; in Victorian anthropology, animism. But in ancient Egypt, Greece and Rome, and among Eskimos, South Sea Islanders, Native Americans and West Africans, the recognition of the image as a living intelligence that plays a governing role in our soul life is simply a basic truth. "Animism" is our Western way of saying that images, places, precious things and natural phenomena are animated, which literally means *ensouled*. So, it seems, that by means of the art of therapy with disordered children, our disordered civilization may be taking its first steps toward the restoration of the sense of a world alive, and that the child appearing in your next counseling session may really be a missionary from heaven.

James Hillman
Thompson, CT
August, 1988

Preface

FOR MANY YEARS as an adolescent and young adult, I struggled painfully with career directions and choices. I was completely at a loss. I hated anything to do with school work but I did love to play! I survived my school at Bedford in England because it had a very strong sports program. The teachers, or "masters" as they were called, were firm and yet caring and actively involved in my development.

In my last year I received a sports injury and was sent to an orthopaedic hospital, located deep in a wood, for surgery and recovery. Every day, the beds were wheeled out onto concrete slabs surrounded by birch trees. It was while lying there that I realized that what I loved most was Nature and being out in Nature. My mind was made up: I would become a forester and go to Canada because they had lots of trees there.

So at eighteen I left England and enrolled in forestry at the University of British Columbia in Vancouver. In addition to science and forestry courses that first year, I discovered the Nature of Literature and the beauty of Joyce, Hardy, Eliot, Yeats and D.H. Lawrence, and I would stay up until two or three in the morning reading. By the end of the year it was clear my heart was in literature, so I changed majors, enrolling in second year Arts with four English courses and a psychology course. Since I came from England in the late 1950s, psychology was a new field that I had never really heard about before, but the word was out around campus that Don Sampson was the most stimulating professor at the university. In that year my English professors somehow killed literature for me, but Don showed me a new, fascinating world and I decided to become a psychologist.

For my master's degree, Don directed me to a child clinical psychology program at San Jose State University in California. At this time, the university had a child guidance clinic attached to the department and a wonderful set of fully equipped play therapy rooms. For two years I trained there and later took my first job as a child psychotherapist at Ming Quong Children's Center in Los Gatos, California.

Here I came under the tutelage of Dr. Thomas Parker, Jungian analyst and past-president of the C. G. Jung Institute of San Francisco. Thomas opened the world of image and symbol and taught me about the Nature of the Unconscious. After four years of intensive clinical work and supervision, I returned to England to do my doctorate and to finish my Jungian training. When these tasks were completed I was ready to branch out on my own.

I was fascinated by the challenge of trying to adapt and implement some Jungian approaches in both developmental and remedial ways with students, teachers and other school counselors. Hence I decided to move from the child guidance system into the public school system and to work as a school counselor.

Working in the public school system presents quite a challenge for a Jungian analyst, but this challenge is a bit like working with one's own unconscious: one is always dealing with the struggle between the so-called "developed" and "undeveloped" sides. Trying to help hurt, angry, depressed, dying, psychotic and at times physically and sexually abused children survive, grow and learn in the school setting, I had to bridge the gap between their damaged emotional and instinctual world and the press of the collective consciousness of the school: the curriculum, the teachers and the students' parents. This was no easy task, and at times I felt caught between the needs of the child and the needs of the teacher: "Fix this kid. He's wrecking my whole class."

This book consists of a collection of eleven papers written, by myself or with my graduate students, over a ten-year period (1977–1987) of working with children and adolescents. It focuses on a Jungian approach to children in which the therapist provides the "safe and protected space" for treatment and the appropriate materials. Healing occurs within this context through relationship both to the therapist and to the expressive media. Much emotion is experienced through action, image and fantasy activities. Problems are expressed, traumas enacted, pain felt, and eventually reparation and transformation occur. The materials—paint, pencil, crayons, toys, sand and clay—are important vehicles facilitating expression, movement and growth, as are the acts of creation, imagination, play and drama. Through these activities a child often moves from initial loss, pain and hopelessness to self-control, flexible mastery and humor. The act of "doing" in the presence of the therapist seems to repair broken images and lead to healing.

Vancouver, Canada
Spring, 1988

Acknowledgments

I AM INDEBTED to my senior graduate students who have worked with me on many of the projects mentioned in this book over the past ten years. My thanks go out to them and especially to Pat Berry, Judi Bertoia, Joanne Crandall, Suzanne Elliott, Adam Horvath, Doug Jackson, Doug Lee, Marilyn MacVicar, Nancy Mcleod, Judy Moon, Judith Snider, Mary Stuart, and Frank Thompson.

Much of the material has been published in article format elsewhere. In three of the chapters my students were first author: Judi Bertoia in "Spontaneous Drawings in Counseling Seriously Ill Children"; Judith Snider in "Earth, Fire, Water and Sun: Archetypal Art Education with School Children"; and Frank Thompson in "Common Symbols of Children in Art Counseling." In chapter two, "Serial Drawing," Suzanne Elliott wrote the case study for the "partially directed approach." I am also grateful to Mrs. Mary Williams of the Society for Analytical Psychology, London, for her insights and help in the preparation of "Serial Story Writing."

Special thanks to Bay Gumboc for the hours of typing; Ed Montgomery for the fine photographic prints; Lyn Cowan and Mary Helen Sullivan for the editorial help; Doug and Carol, parents of Caroyl Lenette Lindsay, for permission to use her picture on the front cover; and to all of the students for their drawings.

Other acknowledgments include:

Facilitating Emotional and Symbolic Communication in Young Children. Allan, J. (1978). *Journal of Canadian Association for Young Children* 4: 8-19. Copyright 1978. The Canadian Association for Young Children. Adapted with permission.

Serial Drawing: A Jungian Approach with Children. Allan, J. (1988). New York: Wiley & Sons. Copyright 1988. John Wiley & Sons. Adapted with permission. Pages 118-25. Copyright 1984. American Association for Counseling and Development. Adapted with permission.

The Rosebush: A Visualization Strategy for Possible Identification of Child Abuse. Allan, J., and Crandall, J. (1986). *Elementary School Guidance and Counseling* 21: 44-51. Copyright 1986. American

Association for Counseling and Development. Adapted with permission.

Counseling Seriously Ill Children: Use of Spontaneous Drawing. Bertoia, J., and Allan, J. (1988). *Elementary School Guidance and Counseling* 22: 206–21. Copyright 1988. American Association for Counseling and Development. Adapted with permission.

Earth, Fire, Water and Sun: Archetypal Art Education. Snider, J., and Allan, J. (1985). Paper presented at the Annual Meeting of the Inter-Regional Society of Jungian Analysts, Birmingham, Alabama, October 30, 1985.

Spontaneous and Directed Drawings with Physically and Sexually Abused Children. Allan, J. (1987). Paper presented at the Annual Meeting of the Inter-Regional Society of Jungian Analysts, Austin, Texas, October 31, 1987.

Common Symbols of Children in Art Counseling. Thompson, F., and Allan, J. (1987). *Guidance and Counselling* 2 (5): 24–32. Copyright 1987. Governing Council, University of Toronto. Adapted with permission.

The Use of Fantasy Enactment in the Treatment of an Emerging Autistic Child. Allan, J., and MacDonald, R. (1975). *Journal of Analytical Psychology* 20: 57–68. Copyright 1975. Journal of Analytical Psychology. Adapted with permission. Also parts copyrighted 1986. Chiron Publications. Adapted with permission.

Use of Creative Drama with Acting-Out Sixth and Seventh Grade Boys and Girls. Allan, J. (1977). *Canadian Counsellor* 11: 135–43. Copyright 1977. Canadian Journal of Counselling. Adapted with permission.

Serial Story Writing: A Therapeutic Approach with a Physically Abused Young Adolescent. Allan, J. (1978). *Canadian Counsellor* 12: 132–37. Copyright 1978. Canadian Journal of Counselling. Adapted with permission.

Sandplay. Allan, J., and Berry, P. (1987). *Elementary School Guidance and Counseling* 21: 300–06. Copyright 1987. American Association for Counseling and Development. Adapted with permission.

Part I

ART AND DRAWING

Chapter 1

EMOTIONAL AND SYMBOLIC COMMUNICATION
IN YOUNG CHILDREN:
THEORY AND PRACTICE

Theoretical Framework: A Jungian Approach

FANTASIES ARE OFTEN discouraged as being "silly, childish and unproductive." I think some of this fear and suspicion come from the influence of Freud, who viewed such a style of communication as regressive, infantile and pathological. Freud saw the unconscious as essentially a negative container composed of primitive aggressive and sexual drives that were in need of repression, control and sublimation. The ego was placed in the dominant position of mediator and adaptation to the outer world given utmost importance.

Jung, on the other hand, took a very different point of view and one that led to the split between himself and Freud in 1912. In an "Essay on Two Kinds of Thinking" (later published in *Symbols of Transformation*, Jung, 1956), he analyzed the symbolism in the diary of a young girl and gave credence to both rational, verbal, directed thinking and non-rational, non-directed modes of communication. He saw the former as the logical part which helps one adapt to the outer world and operate in terms of causal sequences. The latter he viewed as effortless, spontaneous, and conducive to fantasy images and symbols.

Concerning fantasy images, Jung felt that Freud's view was too narrow and restrictive. Certainly, fantasy productions can be pathological, but on another level Jung thought that symbol production also represented the psyche's attempt to grow and, in the case of trauma, to heal itself. In other words, Jung (1964) believed that, if one took the images and symbols of the unconscious as

3

valid and related to them as such, then the inner life would unfold and develop.

In Jung's view the structure of the personality has three layers: the Ego, the Personal Unconscious and the Collective Unconscious. By Ego he meant the center of consciousness, the "I" that we are aware of and know; the Personal Unconscious contains the repressed, suppressed and undeveloped drives, instincts and unacceptable desires, acts and memories beginning in infancy (in part similar to Freud's Id); and the contents of the Collective Unconscious reflect archetypal processes. By describing the Collective Unconscious as the "storehouse" of common knowledge and experience accumulated by humankind during the struggle for survival over the past three million years, Jung meant that, as people have faced the same crisis situations through time, the psyche has developed "inner" solutions to these problems. These "unconscious solutions" are often expressed symbolically through dream images and daydreams. These solutions then must be integrated into Ego consciousness. One way to help this integration, Jung felt, was to make the symbols or images tangible by such activities as painting, drawing, writing (poems, stories), clay sculptures, dance or mime.

The central organizing principle of the Collective Unconscious Jung termed the archetype of the "Self." The Self is similar to the archetypal God-image in each of us, striving toward helping us fulfill our potential and toward unity of the whole personality. It is the substratum of the psyche from which dreams are produced, and the knowledge of the Self is expressed in pictures, images and in the language of symbolism and metaphors. Unlike the Ego, the Self is not bound by the conventions of time and place. It is concerned with the "now" and feelings of immortality, indestructibility and the realm of possibilities and wishes. It is that aspect of us that imagines we "can be everything" and "do everything." It often "ignores" the realm of the Ego and the role of hard work, practice and persistence which are necessary to turn wishes into realities. The Self's primary mode of operation is through the function of intuition, while the Ego operates through logical, deductive thinking processes.

Jung (1964) warned that the Self should not be idealized. The Self has both positive and negative aspects—healing potentials as well as inflationary delusions. The task of psychological growth is to achieve a balanced communication between the Ego and the Self.

It is interesting to note that, over the past ten years, considerable psychophysiological support for these ideas of Jung's seems to be emerging (Ornstein, 1972) and that there is now some evidence that our left-brain hemisphere assumes the Ego functions of consciousness while the right hemisphere governs the symbolic expressions of the Self (Rossi, 1977).

Early Childhood

Extensions of Jung's ideas to early childhood have been made by Fordham (1957), who postulates that the Self exists as an original totality prior to the Ego. At birth the Ego is embedded in the Self as a potentiality, but it does not exist in any functioning capacity. With cortical maturation, the Ego develops and slowly emerges out of the Self to form the center of consciousness. It becomes equated with the "I" that we know, and it helps an individual adapt to the outer world.

The connection between the two has been termed the "Ego–Self" axis (Neumann, 1954), important because it becomes the path of communication between the conscious and unconscious personalities. (In physiological terms, this would be the corpus callosum which connects the two cerebral hemispheres [Bakan, 1976]). In order for the Ego to survive stress and to grow, it needs to maintain its connection with the instinctual roots of the psyche. Damage to this Ego–Self axis leads to feelings of alienation from the Self.

A crucial phase in the development of this axis occurs during the first five years of life. Here, the Ego is slowly formed by what Fordham has called a "process of integration and deintegration." By this he means that a small, weak Ego emerges, is functional for a while, then breaks up (i.e., deintegrates), and later re-forms but in a slightly stronger way. This pattern occurs repeatedly until the age of five or six, by which time a more stable Ego has developed.

This process, Fordham believes, is often manifested in children's drawings where the splattering of dots and fragmentation of objects reflect the deintegration phase, whereas mandalas (circles, squares, triangles) represent the Self in union with the Ego. The circle can be seen as the boundaries of the Ego but refers, at the same time, to the Self (i.e., a state of "congruence"). The mandalas then reflect the development of protective walls which function as intrapsychic means of preventing outbursts and behavioral disintegration. In early childhood, the integration/deintegration phase is most frequently observed during the separation/individuation stage from twelve to thirty months. This phase frequently worries and upsets parents, especially with the first child, because it is characterized by two to three days of calm, followed by two to three days of total chaos and then by the restoration of temporary calm, and so on. The deintegration of the Self and the fragmentation of the immature Ego result in poorly controlled, impulsive and frequently destructive behavior. When the Ego re-constellates, it is as if it has gathered more elements from the Self and in doing so has become stronger. As the Ego becomes organized, impulses become less powerful and a coherent conscious mind comes into existence. A child will now have skills in controlling some impulses and in dealing with the outside world.

Another characteristic of this phase which seems to peak between eighteen and twenty-four months is rapprochement and ambivalence: a child will demand milk but push it away when offered, or will ask to be held but struggle or fight when picked up. Two opposite feelings are expressed simultaneously.

Setting firm limits (immediate and of short duration) at this age is important, because they help to separate the child from the ambivalence of his feelings. Over time, healthy external limits imposed by the parents seem to help the child establish inner controls and to facilitate the emergence of the Ego from the self-centered nature of the unconscious. For example, too few controls can result in very destructive, impulsive and self-centered children. On the other hand, too many controls tend to block and damage the

Ego–Self axis so that a child becomes overly controlled, overly rational and usually obsessive-compulsive with little spontaneity or joy.

In normal children, the period from three to six years is often characterized by considerable movement up and down the Ego–Self axis. This is seen in their rich fantasy play and symbolic activities. When examined closely, this seems to be a period of expression and differentiation of various feeling states. Around three years, children begin to experiment and explore the meaning of various feelings. Feelings and emotions are often expressed through the symbols the child uses. At first, there is often a confusion between inner and outer realities.

Feelings are attributed to outer world objects (trees may be "crying"), and children may start a sentence in the verbal Ego language and finish it in the metaphorical-pictorial language of the Self. This is often confusing to adults unless they are familiar with developmental principles and metaphorical language and can grasp the emotional meaning the symbols have for a child.

In order for the child to maintain contact with the inner world of symbols and feelings, the axis path between the Self and the Ego must be kept open. If the Self is to grow and the Ego is to mature, some form of symbolic expression or outlet is needed. The expressive forms I encourage in work with children are drawings, paintings, clay sculptures, and stories. The language of the Self is that of pictures, images, metaphors and feelings.

There is considerable literature available on verbal communication between children and adults (Ginott, 1972, and Gordon, 1970, in particular) but little in regard to symbolic communication. By this I mean that parents and teachers are not taught or shown how to relate to or to encourage the fantasies and imaginative material of young children. More specifically, I am referring to the "stories" young children tell, their dreams, paintings, clay works and fantasy games. Indeed, from extensive contacts with both teachers and parents, I am led to the conclusion that many adults are often confused and frightened by children's fantasies (Allan, 1975). Part of this fear stems, I believe, from the lack of an adequate framework in which to view this material. In this chapter, I want to give examples of ways in which symbolic communication and expression can be encouraged.

Communication Techniques

Teachers, counselors and day care personnel need to be trained in various communication skills in order to understand the emotional and symbolic expressions of young children. The amount of emotional and symbolic material a child shares is often dependent on the sensitivity and skill of the adult. Over the years, I have found several of the concepts of Axline (1947), Baruch (1949), Ginott (1972) and Gordon (1970) useful. Some of these are:

1. *A belief* that talking with children about their concerns and feelings helps them.

2. *Actively observing, listening to* and *perceiving* what the child is saying or doing. This means being aware of where the child is in-the-here-and-now and how the child is experiencing the world.

3. *The use of re-statements,* i.e., mirroring back to the child the cognitive content of what he or she has just said. The purpose of this is to let the child know that one has heard him or her and to put the ball back into his or her lap so that the child will continue to talk.

4. *The selective use of questions.* It is better to re-state than to ask "why?" As the young child's ego is still immature, it is often hard for him to express why he did something. Usually a question is met with an "I don't know." Instead, one can ask for a description: "What did you do?"

Another approach, when working with children's stories or pictures, is to describe what one sees and to use the symbols or images as the focal point for questions. For example, when describing a picture one might say: "I see a house burning, people running out and a brown bear coming. I wonder what the people are thinking . . . [allow time for the child to talk out] . . . and feeling . . . and what the bear is thinking . . . and feeling . . . and I wonder what happens to the house . . . the people . . . and the bear. . . ."

5. *The use of reflection of feeling* is deeper than a re-statement and captures the underlying feelings. It involves verbalizing back to the child the implicit emotional feeling contained in his or her statement or picture. The purpose of such feeling reflection is to make the unconscious (or sub-conscious) conscious and to show the child that one understands how he or she feels (i.e., to communicate empathy):

> Child: "I hit his face, then his tummy and then I kicked him."
> Adult: "You were really angry at Billy and wanted to hurt him."

6. *The use of self* involves the teacher using her own feelings, intuitions and perceptions and verbalizing these to the child. For example, in the above interactions the teacher could add: "I guess it really upset you when Billy wrecked your block castle. I wonder if there is another way you can let him know how you felt."

Another aspect of the use of self involves the teacher's describing what she sees and then reporting her own feelings: "Johnny, when I see you running around, pulling the girls' hair, yelling and screaming, it upsets me, gives me a headache and makes me angry. I wish you would stop it and go and play with the drums."

7. *The use of effective limits* means the teacher verbalizes her automatic parent function. She clearly defines the limits and the consequences if the child violates them. The consequences should be immediate, of short duration, and designed not to reinforce negative behavior.

A Group Approach for Facilitating Emotional and Symbolic Expression

This group method has been used successfully with children from three on up into the elementary school (Allan and Nairne, 1984). It involves setting aside twenty to forty minutes each week (preferably the same time) for discussing feelings. The teacher selects enough topics for a five- to ten-week period (happiness, fear, loneliness, sadness, anger, love, etc.) which seem to be rele-

9

vant to the children's developmental stage and presents one feeling each week. The format I use has three parts. Here is an illustration using "fear" as the topic.

A. Ask the group, or class as a whole, a series of questions about fear. For best results, the questions should be presented sequentially, and one should move slowly from the general (*a* boy, *a* girl) to the specific ("Have *you* ever felt afraid?"). During this process, I encourage as much discussion as possible by using re-statement and reflection techniques as well as other group interaction skills. It is useful to think of several stimulus questions beforehand, so that when the discussion begins to fade a new question can be raised. Some of these might include:

1. "What is fear?"
2. "How does a boy [or girl] *feel* when he [or she] is frightened or scared?"
3. "What does he [or she] *look like* when scared?" (Get them to describe it and then to show you with their faces and bodies.)
4. "What does a boy or girl *do* when frightened?"
5. "Have *you* ever been afraid?"
6. "What did *you feel like?*"
7. "*Where* did you feel it in your body? Can you show me?"
8. "What did you do?"
9. "What *could you do* next time?"
10. "What was the *scariest moment in your life?*"

Obviously, one should not adhere rigidly to this format but rather use it flexibly, depending on the time available, the quality of group discussion, and the age of the children. Sometimes three to five questions are sufficient.

B. After the discussion and dialogues on fear, ask the children to *draw, paint, or write a story about fear.* You can say:

1. "Can you try to get this feeling of fear down on paper?"
2. "What does fear look like?"
3. "What is scary for you?"
4. "Can you draw or paint a frightening scene?"

C. After the painting activity, you can ask the children to *share their work, to hold it up and to describe it* to the others if they wish. During this phase, the teacher can help by asking:

1. "What's going on in the picture?"
2. "In what way is it scary?"
3. "What happens [i.e., what's the outcome]?"

The purpose of this approach is to help the children (a) become more aware of the different feeling states within them, (b) develop some understanding of and how to handle the feelings (e.g., "What could you do next time?"), (c) share their feelings with other children and see that other children have similar ones, (d) communicate their feelings and concerns with the teacher, and (e) express their feelings symbolically through the use of plastic media. Emotions and thoughts that were not revealed before in the verbal discussion are often explored and shared in the painting stage. Also, such an expression, I believe, reduces tension and hence the need to act out feelings in a destructive way. This is especially so when the teacher or counselor is able to work with the material sensitively and therapeutically.

Examples

The following excerpts from case materials were recorded and transcribed during group discussion and painting sessions with pre-school children.

1. *Kelly, five-year-old girl.* The group discussion has finished, and the children are busy painting. The counselor approaches her.

Counselor	Child	Comments
1. What are you afraid of, Kelly?	2. Nightmares.	
3. What is in your picture?	4. There is a man with a gun on my bed. This is my doll. There's some big hearts. There is blood. There are footsteps [fig. 1.1].	This was a richly painted picture. It was interesting to see that whenever she painted something frightening—the man, the gun, the blood, the footsteps—she placed the hearts and/or a doll near them.
5. How do you feel when you have a nightmare?	6. Scary. I shiver and shake.	

11

7. What do you do?	8. I go into my mummy's bed really quickly.	
9. What would you do next time?	10. Usually my aunt sleeps with me so I don't have to be afraid.	
11. What are you most afraid of?	12. When a ghost flies into your room and the curtains move. That's what makes me most scared.	Child reveals a specific frightening incident.

Comment: With this revelation, the counselor was able to talk with Kelly about how frightening it was to see the curtains move when no one was there and to explain how they often move when the wind blows or when the heat fan is on.

2. *Tara, three and a half years old.* This child was afraid of coming into the pre-school.

Child	Teacher	Comments
1. I'm afraid of snakes [draws some lines]. Mum isn't so I will talk to her.	2. Snakes. Anything else?	She probes.
3. Bears and things.	4. Are you ever afraid to come to school?	Her probe is more specific.
5. Yes, sometimes it hurts.		Supervisor is inadvertently called away. Tara keeps drawing. Another supervisor passes by. Tara says:
6. I'm drawing something.	7. So I see.	An acknowledgment.
8. I'm drawing my school.	9. Your school.	Simple re-statement.
10. I'm drawing my mummy bringing me to school and I don't want to come in. Look at this [a huge, crayoned black area]. I cry [fig. 1.2].	11. It looks very dark and it makes you sad to come here.	Notice how the child goes deeper.
12. Yes, it's because I'm scared.	13. It's frightening leaving your mother and coming to school where you don't know many people yet.	A reflection and an added interpretation.
14. Yes.	15. You know me now and we can be friends.	Use of self. Teacher personalizes the interaction and uses herself as a "transitional" person.
16. Yes, I'm not afraid now.		

FIG. 1.1   Doll, hearts and blood

FIG. 1.2   My school is dark

3. Carla, five years old.

Child	Teacher	Comments
1. I'm afraid of the buzzer I have in my room.	2. You're afraid of the buzzer?	The teacher has no idea what "the buzzer" is, at this point, and simply re-states.
3. I haven't wet for a long time.	4. You feel good when you don't wet.	Teacher now understands and uses a reflection of feeling in order to encourage the child to continue talking.
5. If I wet the buzzer goes on. It makes me scared. I don't like it. My mum says I nearly jump to the ceiling when it goes off.	6. It really frightens you and makes your body jump.	Another reflection.
7. Yes, like this [child throws her arms straight up in the air, fingers spread out and taut].	8. Can you draw that for me?	The purpose of this is to provide the child with both an outlet for her feelings (i.e., the drawing) and with *time in the feeling* (i.e., the duration of the drawing), where the Ego might both allow expression and gain some mastery over the feelings in order to disclose more.
9. [She spends a long time on the drawing. Draws herself in a startled response, attached by a cord to the buzzer. Buzzer is drawn in great detail, and she talks while drawing.] Oh, I have to be sad. I have to get up and go to the bathroom. Mum is proud of me when I don't wet but not when I do [fig. 1.3].	10. You feel your mum doesn't like you when you wet?	Teacher reflects deeper feeling.
11. Yes [long silence].	12. You want her to be proud of you.	Teacher reflects the wish.
13. Yes.		

Comment: The teacher had had no idea of this problem before. Subsequently, she spoke to the child's mother and found that Carla's older sister had been a bed wetter until she was fourteen and was "cured" by the buzzer system. To insure that this would

FIG. 1.3   Me and the buzzer

not happen with Carla, the parents decided to use the buzzer while she was still young. The teacher explained that she felt Carla was actually too young, that "accidents" would occur and that the electric shock seemed very frightening and possibly damaging to the child and to the mother–daughter relationship. As an alternative, the teacher said she would encourage Carla to get involved in sand and water play, thus providing her with a symbolic outlet for working through this developmental task. Sure enough, after a few weeks of sand and water play the bed-wetting issue was resolved.

4. *Millie, five years old.*

Child	Teacher	Comments
1. One time when I was at my old house, a baby-sitter was with me and she was in the bathroom and someone knocked at the door and I said, "Come in," and instead of my dad it was a monster.	2. Oh, no! What did you do?	Notice how the story starts on the realistic Ego level and then suddenly drops down to the symbolic (Self) level.

15

3. I jumped out of the window.

4. How did you feel?

5. I feeled scary. I ran around. I took my bike out the window with me, I ride it really fast, and you know what, he slipped over a car, and he got runned over, and you know what happened again? Another monster came, and he was a giant one. And he ran fast but he couldn't catch me. So, he got runned over too, and then ANOTHER, NOTHER one, and he was a bigger one, and he catched up to me and he—the police came, because he had a gun, the monster, and the police heared shooting so he came and took the monster away. He took him to jail. He took the mask off and guess who it was? My dad. And I asked him why he was trying to scare me.

6. And what did your dad say?

Observe how the Ego attempts to handle the "scary" feeling by "killing it off" (i.e., by repression) and how the feeling ("monster") keeps on returning with greater intensity because of the repression of feeling.

7. He said he forgot why.

8. And how did you feel when you found out it was your daddy?

Supervisor attempts to focus.

9. I feeled funny inside me and then we both went back to my old house.

The feelings expressed during the story-telling phase were continued but with greater depth in the painting phase which followed immediately. Millie's comments on the three pictures she painted follow:

Picture 1: "My Dad." (The picture had good form with clearly defined body boundaries [in blue] and red splotches around the face.)

> *Her comments were:* "He was at my house. He knocked at the door and I said, 'Who is it?' It was my dad. When I opened the door it was a ghost like that with lots of blood running down

[fig. 1.4]. I was scared and I screamed and I jumped right out of the door."

The teacher observed: "When Millie finished this picture, she moved away from the easel, put her arm over her eyes and said: 'I'm scared, I'm scared of my picture.'"

Teacher: "The monster in the picture scares you?"

Millie: "Yes, it's scary. I want to do another one."

Picture 2: "A Monster." (This picture [fig. 1.5] had much less form—just a blue head and neck, no body and more red paint.)

> *Her comments were:* "He's happy. . . . No, he's a scary one. A monster with only one mouth and blood coming down a whole bunch." (Notice the Ego's initial attempt to deny the affect [he's happy] but how the feeling breaks through.)

Picture 3: "Blood." (The form, as represented previously by blue, was now non-existent in this picture. The main effect—a yellow, blurred face area with red [blood] all over it [fig. 1.6]).

> *Her comments were:* "This one has a whole bunch of yellow eyes and lots and lots of blood."
>
> *The teacher's comments were:* "Once Millie finished this third picture she became relaxed, taking off her apron and saying: 'That's it. It's done.' She went over and started to play with other children and was happy for the rest of the day."

Comment: Discussing this story with the teacher made apparent that there had been a lot of violence in Millie's home and that she had seen her father shoot her mother. There had been blood, and the police had come and taken the father away. On one level, the story reflects the psyche's (i.e., inner Self's) attempt to help Millie deal with this trauma, understand the two sides of her father's personality ("My Dad" and "A Monster") and to express some of the repressed pain about the violence she had witnessed. It seems that this emotional abreaction through painting was necessary in order for the introjected feelings to leave Millie. At a later date, the

17

FIG. 1.4   My Dad

FIG. 1.5   A monster

teacher talked with Millie about how hard it must be to deal with the two conflicting images of her father—his "good side" and his "monster side." Notice how in resolving psychological pain one enters the feeling—in this case, scariness—to move through it and to come out on the other side of it. Millie was noticeably relieved once she had done her three pictures.

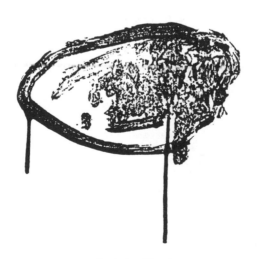

FIG. 1.6   Blood

Chapter 2

SERIAL DRAWING:
A JUNGIAN APPROACH WITH CHILDREN

SERIAL DRAWING IS a therapeutic approach whereby the counselor meets on a regular basis with the child and simply asks the child to "draw-a-picture." Over time a relationship forms, problems are expressed symbolically in the drawings, and healing and resolution of inner conflicts can occur.

Background

The theoretical underpinnings of this approach are based on the work of C. G. Jung. During the latter days of the First World War, Jung (1965) wrote that he:

> sketched every morning in a notebook a small circular drawing, a mandala, which seemed to correspond to my inner situation at the time. With the help of these drawings, I could observe my psychic transformations from day to day. . . . I had to abandon the idea of the superordinate position of the ego. . . . I had to let myself be carried along by the current, without a notion of where it would lead me. (pp. 195-96)

Throughout his life Jung continued to draw and paint, write and illustrate his dreams, and carve in wood and stone. He felt that psychological health was a delicate balance between the demands of the outer world and the needs of the inner world. To him, the expressive arts represented an important avenue to the inner world of feelings and images. He came to see the unconscious mind not only as a repository of repressed emotions but also as a source of health and transformation. In time of stress one could turn inward toward the unconscious for dreams and images that carried within them the potential, or seeds, for healing. His was not a reductive method of analysis but rather a synthetic, teleological point of view. He was interested in where a person's inner life was leading him or her. From this framework, the psychotherapist does not necessarily analyze the images of the client but rather encourages the client to "make" the images and to follow them as they unfold. To a certain extent, it is as if the ego moves aside a little to allow unconscious movements and images to have ascendency over the conscious mind.

Jung (1966) believed that the establishment of a therapeutic alliance and rapport activated the healing potential that is embedded in the human psyche. He saw this healing potential as part of the "archetype of the self" which leads a person on the path to individuation or toward the fulfillment of potential. When activated by the therapeutic alliance, the archetype takes the client where the client needs to go. For example, in play therapy children will often spontaneously work on fantasy themes that have direct relevance to their psychological struggles. And so it is true with drawings.

Serial Drawing

Serial drawing refers to drawing every week in the presence of the counselor. In talking about drawings and paintings, Jung (1959) emphasized the importance of viewing them "in series" over time rather than just analyzing one or two pictures. When a child draws in the presence of the therapist on a regular basis, then the healing potential is activated, conflicts expressed and resolved, and the therapist can gain a clearer and more accurate view of the unconscious "at work." The time–place variables act as a sanctuary space, a time out of ordinary time, which, together with a positive therapeutic alliance, foster psychological growth and transformation.

From a Jungian perspective these conditions activate in the unconscious mind the drive toward healing. Fantasies and images are produced which, if symbolized or concretized (i.e., expressed in tangible form through play enactment, drawing, clay, writing, etc.), facilitate psychological growth. The 8½-by-11-inch piece of white paper becomes the "safe place" onto which projections are placed, while the symbols and images become the "containers" for various emotions, thus allowing feelings to be expressed. With this safe expression, movement occurs in the unconscious and new images (feelings) are produced.

Each child moves at his or her own pace, depending on the nature of the trauma or psychological struggle and the child's ego strength. Though general patterns have been observed (Allan, 1978a), some children will start by producing images of pain, others images of reparation and healing, while others show only very stereotyped drawings. Some children spend a long time on painful images, others move directly into images of healing (seemingly no longer needing to deal with the pain), while others appear to get stuck in powerful, ambivalent clashes between the desire to grow and the wish to destroy. These unique patterns only become apparent over time, hence the serial nature of this treatment approach.

Symbolic Themes

Quite often in serial drawing, a child will pick up on one symbolic theme and use it throughout many of the drawings. The image is seldom used in a perseverative way; rather, the image changes in its form or function. Many times there is a movement from damage and violation to repair and healthy functioning. For example, Pam, six years old and sexually abused, constantly drew bedrooms and bathrooms with people enacting sexual intercourse and showing genitalia. At the end of treatment, there were still bedrooms and bathrooms, but people were sleeping each in his or her own separate bed, the rooms were tidy, and the lights were on. Luci, a psychotic five year old, thought she was a seagull. She carried around a seagull feather in her hand and twirled it in front of her eyes. At first she drew herself as a seagull (fig. 2.1), then herself as supergirl with seagull wings and one feather sticking out (fig. 2.2), then herself as a girl with a seagull flying above her (fig. 2.3), and finally herself as an Indian princess with a feather tucked into her headband (fig. 2.4). Note the transformation as she separates herself (i.e., her ego) out from an overidentification with one aspect of the archetype of the Self (i.e., herself as seagull).

Joey, eleven years old, very quiet, withdrawn and with facial tics, drew a tiny house surrounded by giant hills. Over the weeks, the house moved from the background to the middle of the page and the hills diminished in size. The house then became houses, the houses villages and towns, and finally after six months he drew Manhattan. The whole sheet of paper was full of skyscrapers. At this point he started to talk. Referring to the drawing he said, "This picture is like my dad. These buildings lean over me. Press down on me just like my dad. They suffocate me. He suffocates me. He kisses me, lies on top of me, squeezes my bum and makes me touch him. I hate it. I HATE HIM!" At this point, Joey exploded into a fit of rage and weeping. This led to a disclosure of sexual abuse, and after it came major improvements. This vignette showed how one child used this method and how one particular symbol, a tiny home away in the distance (i.e., deep within the unconscious), slowly surfaced week after week until it was in the forefront of consciousness ("Manhattan") and led to a verbal self-disclosure.

Stages in Serial Drawing

When counselors have used serial drawing with mildly to moderately disturbed children in the public school system, three main stages have been noted: initial, middle, and termination. Each stage seems to be characterized by or to reflect certain typical images or themes.

In the initial stage (first to fourth sessions), the drawings seem to (a) give a view of the child's internal world, often showing images that reflect a cause of his or her problems, (b) reflect loss of inter-

FIG. 2.1   Luci as a seagull

FIG. 2.2   Supergirl

FIG. 2.3   People chasing me

FIG. 2.4   Indian princess

nal control and the presence of feelings of despair and hopelessness, and (c) offer a vehicle for establishing the initial rapport with the counselor. The counselor is often incorporated into the actual drawing in symbolic form as a friendly giant, helicopter pilot, doctor, or nurse.

In the middle stage (fifth to eighth sessions), the drawing content seems to reflect (a) an expression of an emotion in its pure form, (b) the struggle between opposites ("good" vs. "bad") and the isolation of ambivalent feelings, (c) the deepening of the relationship between the child and the helper. At the end of this phase, the child often uses the drawing as (d) a bridge to talk directly about a painful issue or to disclose a secret.

In the termination stage (ninth to twelfth sessions), the child tends to draw (a) images that reflect a sense of mastery, self-control, and worth, (b) scenes reflecting positive imagery (i.e., an absence of war, violence, and damage), (c) a central self symbol (i.e., self-portrait or mandala forms), (d) humorous scenes, (e) pictures reflecting a detachment from the helper.

Other Media in the Serial Approach

Though the focus here is on drawing, the method works equally well with other forms of creative expression. The task facing the counselor is to find the right medium for each child. With some children it is sandplay (Allan and Berry, 1987); others, drama (Allan, 1977); others, fantasy enactment (Allan, 1986; Allan and MacDonald, 1975). Some children work best with painting (Thompson and Allan, 1985), others in clay (Allan and Clark, 1985), while others through creative writing (Allan, 1978b; Buttery and Allan, 1981).

Setting

Serial drawing has been used in a variety of settings from residential care to day care (Allan, 1978c) and from private practice to counseling in the schools. In many ways it is ideally suited to the school system where counselors are often faced with overwhelming case loads (Allan, Doi, and Reid, 1979; Allan and Barber, 1986), because the method requires only a short session per week per child. Some children, in acute crisis, might need to be seen every day. The methods of serial drawing described next and the case studies mentioned below were all conducted in the public elementary school system where the author works both as a counselor and a counselor educator.

Methods

Serial drawing involves seeing a child alone for twenty to twenty-five minutes once a week and asking the child to "draw-a-picture." White paper (8½-by-11-inch) and pencil are the only requirements. The counselor can say to the child something like:

> Mary, I'm Dr. Allan, the school counselor. Schools want to help children not only with school work but also with their lives, their feelings, and with things that trouble them. That's my job in the school: to help children. Your teacher [parent] told me that life in the classroom [at home] seemed hard for you right now, and she thought that coming to see me would help you. Often children like to draw and talk when they come to see me. Drawing and talking seem to help children feel better, overcome problems, and enjoy life more. Your teacher suggested I see you every Tuesday from 10:00 to 10:20. You can draw or talk about whatever you wish. What we talk about is private. Just between you and me unless something is against the law. I will keep your pictures here in my office in this file. [Show the child the file.] Usually I write your name, date, and title of the picture on the back and keep it safe in here [i.e., the file]. When life goes better and when you and I have finished seeing each other, then I will give the file, with all of the pictures, back to you. Do you have any questions? [At this point, I usually slide the paper and pencil across the table and slightly toward the child.]

The key ingredients here are (a) establishing rapport, (b) identifying the helping role, (c) placing treatment in the context of school life, (d) suggesting that talking and drawing help, (e) identifying time and place variables and the counselor's connection to the teacher, (f) the storing of the pictures (i.e., containing, protecting, and valuing the "products"), (g) stating that the drawings will be returned to the child later, and (h) offering the child a chance to talk and question.

Because the treatment time is short, crayons, ruler, and eraser can be kept out of view. Crayons seem to detract from the process because the child will tend to spend a lot of time shading. Coloring and shading both have therapeutic value, but in this brief counseling context they should not be promoted. However, if a child asks for crayons or an eraser, then provide them. Obviously there must be some flexibility in the use of this approach. Try to use the same office or, if this consistency isn't possible in some schools, use a quiet corner of a classroom or library. A new piece of paper is placed in front of the child each time. Some children may ask for the drawing and spend five or six sessions reworking one picture. If children ask to take the picture out of the office with them, reflect their wish but add that it is important to keep it in the file (i.e., boundaries, limits, and protection of the psychological material are important for transformation). Try to discover the importance and meaning of this act (taking the picture out), dialogue about it, but if the impasse is maintained, make a photocopy of the picture and try to keep the original for the file.

During the sessions, the counselor sits near or beside the child. The counselor does not talk much, in the beginning stage, unless the child initiates it. Introverted children will tend to work silently on their pictures, and this should be respected. Extroverted children are often full of action sounds and like to talk a lot while drawing. Respond minimally to them so the focus is placed on the drawing. The counselor does not initiate any conversation or take any notes, but observes the child, how the child approaches the drawing, the placement of the figures and the types of images, symbols, and themes that emerge in the child's pictures.

The counselor needs to be sensitive to the "subtle body" (Schwartz-Salant, 1986), to the invisible feeling-toned space that develops between himself or herself and the child. As the child draws, there is movement in his or her unconscious mind, old feelings are expressed and new ones rise to the surface, the transference–countertransference develops, and the counselor needs to be aware of the subtle feeling changes in the child and in himself or herself. This helps the counselor understand the child's psychological struggles and to make silent hypotheses. This silent understanding and acceptance seem to help the child move forward. Sometimes a child may become "stuck" with a certain theme which will be repeated time and time again without any apparent movement. When this occurs, the counselor may have to take a more active role in verbalizing or interpreting the conflict, as in the case of Billie, below.

Counselor's Behavior during the Sessions

The counselor's verbal and non-verbal behaviors are all critically important to the success of the method. Most importantly, the counselor must believe that the method will help the child and that the activity has important psychological benefits. The counselor provides an environment that reflects unconditional positive regard, helps establish trust, and enables the child to draw and talk. As the children vary so much in their styles of interaction, the counselor will have to be flexible. At first, the counselor needs to try to follow the child's direction. If the child talks while drawing, the counselor responds, sometimes by reflecting feelings and sometimes by answering questions. If the child—involved with the drawing—is very quiet, then the counselor remains quiet, attends to the child, the images, and his or her own feelings.

At the end of each session, the counselor asks the child, "Does the picture tell a story? Can you tell me what's going on in the picture? Does the picture have a title?" Sometimes it helps to obtain amplifications by asking, "What went on in the story before this picture? What happens next?" Also, in this termination phase of the session, it is legitimate for the counselor to ask about anything unusual that he or she has observed during the drawing time. For example, "Mike, while you were drawing the house, I noticed you spent a long time on the doorknob. I wonder if you could tell me what you were thinking while you were drawing and shading it? What does the doorknob do (or mean to you)?" Questions should be left to the end so that they do not interrupt the flow of the child's drawing activity. The drawing is more than just drawing; it is an opportunity for the child psychologically to "work through" some inner representations, issues, or conflicts.

Specific Serial Drawing Techniques

There are three main techniques: non-directive, directive, and partially directive. Directiveness in this context refers only to whether or not the counselor suggests a topic or symbol for the child to draw.

Non-Directive. Some children come to the sessions, see the paper and pencil, and start drawing even before the counselor talks. These children readily respond to the counselor and the therapeutic environment and seem to know what they want or need to draw. They begin psychological work right away and in the early stages apparently need the counselor only as a witness to their drawings. With these children, it is important to use a non-directive approach because they are already connected to their own curative process. They intuitively know where they need to go and what they need to draw.

Directive. Some children seem withdrawn, stuck, trapped in stereotyped images, confused and very uncertain of themselves. A suggestion of what to draw often helps these children get under way with their own work. With these children, the session can be started with a House-Tree-Person test series (Buck, 1948) and continued with other directed drawings until the children seem ready to draw on their own, reject or substitute their own images, or until the counselor feels it is no longer appropriate to direct the process. As in this example, with a very angry child—"Could you draw an exploding volcano?"—the direction is not made randomly, but is based on the counselor's psychological assessment of a central emotion that the child is currently struggling with or an image or symbol that seems to have special meaning to the child at this moment in his or her life.

Partially Directive. Sometimes one particular symbol has a special relevance to the child. The child attaches to or communicates this image very early on to the counselor. The image is often broken or damaged or represents a symbol of wholeness or health to the child. This symbol seems to represent a central force in his or her development. It could be anything that has special meaning to the child: a house, a garage, a flower, a tree, a worm, the underground, the sun, a cage, a dog, etc. In the partially directive technique, every four to six weeks the counselor asks the child to draw that particular symbol. The counselor can simply state at the start of the session, "Simon, I've been thinking about the cage today. I wonder if you could draw me a picture of it. I wonder what has been happening to it since the last time you drew it?" Four to six weeks seems to be an optimum time in which the psyche registers change and for a child to develop a slightly new attitude or relationship to a key symbolic theme.

Case Examples

Non-Directive Approach

Some children seem to know intuitively what they need to draw and how best to heal themselves. These children can make significant improvement in ten to twelve weeks, and in retrospect their drawings seem to go through three phases: initial, middle, and termination, with each phase being characterized by distinct themes and images. For optimum facilitation, the counselor's responses and actions must be different in each of these stages. The protocols of two children, Sam and Billie, illustrate these stages and themes and the counselor's response patterns.

Sam (six years) and Billie (seven years) both came from families where the parents had divorced, and both demonstrated severe behavioral problems in their classrooms. Sam had moved about

31

fourteen times in his life, and Billie's mother had just deserted the family, breaking off all contact with him.

Initial Stage (first to fourth sessions). These pictures seem to:

1. *Give a view of the child's internal world.* For example, Sam's drawings depicted long-distance moving trucks smashing into little cars, killing people, crossing the lane dividers of freeways, and crashing into houses on the other side (fig. 2.5). Billie's pictures showed "The Whole World on Fire" with volcanoes everywhere, earthquakes cracking and tearing the world apart, houses being blown up, people trapped in them, rockets and bombs exploding. The central themes in both cases were devastation and disaster.

2. *Reflect the feelings of hopelessness.* The themes of the first three drawings often tend to reflect the overwhelming and incapacitating effect of the trauma on the child's sense of competency and mastery. Helplessness is clearly revealed in Billie's drawing as he depicts himself trapped in a mountain during an

FIG. 2.5   Freeway crash

earthquake (fig. 2.6). There may be some rudimentary attempt on the part of the hero figures to try to escape destruction or to do something positive. However, in this phase, the negative or destructive forces always win. With Billie, the trapped figure got out of the mountain but was killed by a rock. With Sam, crashes always occurred on the freeway.

3. *Represent a vehicle for establishing the initial contact with the helper.* Children frequently use the drawings to start to build a relationship with the counselor. Sam began to draw many helicopters and airplanes flying about the freeway. He also drew road maps and mazes and began to challenge the counselor to find his way out: "Bet you can't get out of that one?" (fig. 2.7). Billie kept asking his counselor, "Can you guess what I'm drawing?" It seems that underneath the children were asking, "Do you understand me? Do you know what has happened to me? Are you smart enough to help me?" Billie also always asked his counselor to write her name on the front of his drawing.

FIG. 2.6   Trapped in a mountain quake

33

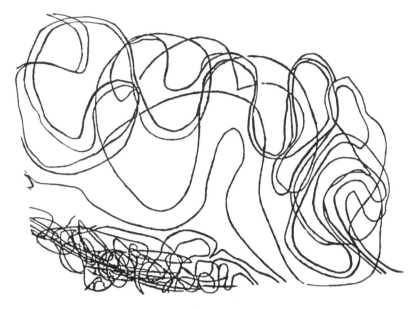

FIG. 2.7   Maze challenge

Middle Stage (fifth to eighth sessions). These drawings tend to reflect:

1.   *An expression of an emotion in its pure form.* In this phase, it is as if certain painful feelings are separated out from other feelings and expressed in pure form. For example, Sam continued to draw freeways, but showed his depression by drawing "the truck disappearing down a great hole in the middle of the road." With Billie, one main focus was rage—a giant pouring out a mass of fury and anger from his mouth (fig. 2.8), while a later picture reflected grief and sadness: "an army of ants carried a huge teardrop off to a safe place so it could break open without hurting anyone in the two houses below" (fig. 2.9).

2.   *A struggle with ambivalent feelings.* Later drawings equally contained positive and negative forces: "a log, hurtling toward earth, containing explosives but prevented from crashing by a thousand birds holding it up" (fig. 2.10). In another drawing, Billie showed "a mean tree throwing a spear at Jack Pumpkinhead

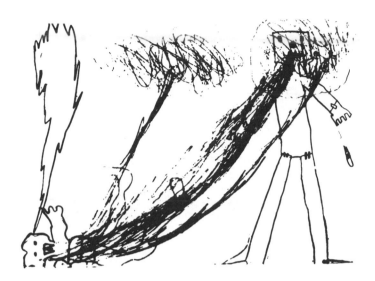

FIG. 2.8   Angry giant

FIG. 2.9   Giant teardrop

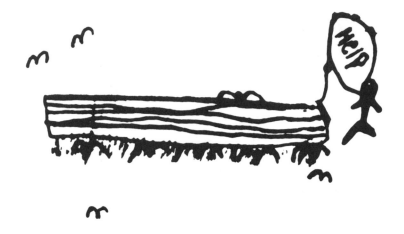

FIG. 2.10   Explosive log

but a snowman quickly puts a shield over Jack's head which protects him" (fig. 2.11).

3. *A deeper relationship to the helper.* The counselor now tends to be incorporated into the drawing as a positive, helpful image. Sam began drawing "a man flying planes with logs and supplies to repair the holes in the roads" (fig. 2.12). Billie drew a "friendly giant rescuing a boy from the floods that came to earth after the fire" (fig. 2.13).

4. *The disclosure of a deep issue.* With the establishment of the therapeutic relationship, the child begins to trust the counselor and shares some deep feelings and thoughts. Sam wrote the words "I feel sad" (fig. 2.14) and talked about his grief over moving so many times, how he did not like it, how it hurt to make and lose friends, and how frightening he found his new school. Billie started to draw "help," several in one picture (fig. 2.15), and he revealed how the hero in the picture "had wanted to kill himself a year ago" (i.e., when his mother left) and how "he still thought

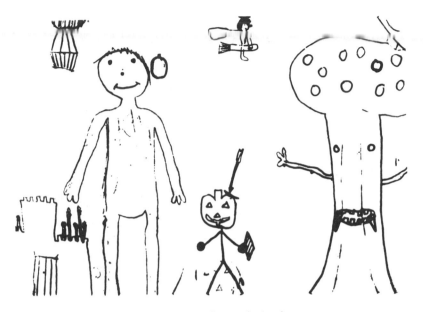

FIG. 2.11   Jack Pumpkinhead

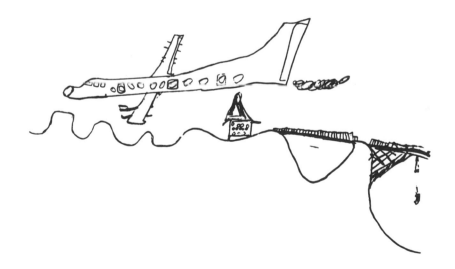

FIG. 2.12   Plane brings supplies

FIG. 2.13   Rescuing the boy

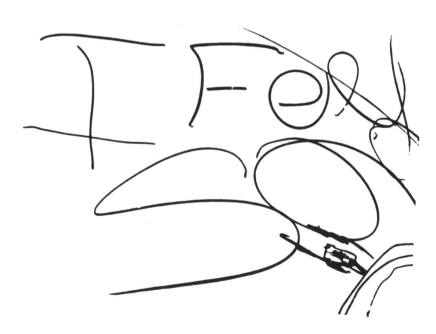

FIG. 2.14   "I feel sad"

about killing himself sometimes." At this point in the therapeutic relationship, it is important that the counselor begin to relate the content of the drawings directly to the child's life (i.e., to interpret). For example, in the above situation: "I guess when your mother left home it really hurt you and at times you wished you were dead and wouldn't have to be in so much pain. I'm glad you are telling me about these feelings."

Termination Stage (ninth to twelfth sessions).

Once the deeper feelings and pain have been expressed symbolically and/or shared verbally, there tends to be rapid movement toward a resolution. The drawings now show:

1. *Images of mastery, self-control and worth.* The drawings begin to reflect feelings of competency and coping. The freeway traffic in Sam's drawings was back to normal; all the cars and trucks were running smoothly, the road dividers in place, the

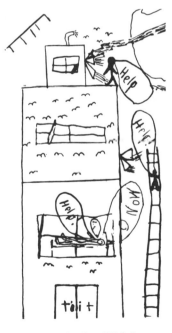

FIG. 2.15   "Help"

39

repairs to the road finished; and there were even "control towers" to regulate and keep a watchful eye on the traffic.

2.   *The emergence of positive imagery.* There are no wars or explosions, and fewer conflicts now. Billie drew "Hawaiian Scenes"—a big, bright sun, coconut and pineapple trees, smiles on everyone's faces (fig. 2.16).

3.   *Humor.* Dangerous "forces" are now related to humorously. Billie re-drew the dangerous log of session seven that was going to blow the world up, but this time there was a swordfish cutting it up into tiny pieces, and next to it a pile of used and broken swordfish blades that had been blunted in the process (fig. 2.17).

4.   *A central self-symbol.* Sam drew a series of self-portraits: a big smile on his face with a cigar sticking out of the corner of his mouth (fig. 2.18). Often, these drawings are protected by a frame or border. There is, too, the emergence of mandala forms such as a square, circle, or triangle around the central image. Billie drew his "grandmother" lying on a towel in Hawaii; she was in a bikini and

FIG. 2.16   Hawaiian Scenes

FIG. 2.17 Swordfish cuts log

FIG. 2.18 "Me"

near her was a dish of pineapple and coconut. The rectangular border of the towel protected her and reflected the sunlight in rays—so that the "grandmother" was highlighted in the drawing (fig. 2.19).

These drawings reflect the internalization of positive images. Sam now carried around inside himself a positive self-image (albeit slightly omnipotent! [fig. 2.20]), and Billie re-established connection to the mother archetype (Neumann, 1974) in the form of his inner "grandmother."

5. *A detachment from the helper.* In this termination stage, the child now withdraws some libido from the counselor. For example, in the picture of Sam's self-portrait, there was a tiny picture of the helper in the background. The helper no longer had the prominence of the helicopter pilot in the earlier drawings. Billie had always asked the counselor to write her name on every picture he drew, first on the front, then the back; but in the last drawings this was not requested.

After these types of drawings, the child usually says, "I don't want to come any more," and at this point the counselor, too, becomes aware that there is no need to continue seeing the child. There is a feeling of resolution both internally and externally. Positive inner images ("introjects") have been restored, and behavioral problems in the classroom that led to the referral are often no longer present.

The Counselor's Role

The question of the degree of counselor-initiated activity is a difficult one and probably ultimately depends on the counselor's own unique personality style. At first it is important that the counselor say very little, in the belief that understanding and meaning occur symbolically on an unconscious level. However, if the child is in great pain and struggling, and if the counselor feels the need to strengthen the attachment bond and transference, then linkages can be made from the drawings to the therapeutic relationship or to outer world situations. This can be done when the counselor sees that the child is stuck in repetitious cycles or when interpretation is needed to reduce pain or anxiety. Too much questioning,

FIG. 2.19   Grandmother

FIG. 2.20   "Me as superman"

reflection, or interpretation, however, can sometimes block the spontaneous healing process of the child.

Such linkages or interpretations should be left to the end of the session and then used in conjunction with the content of the drawings as the first bridge into the empathic response. For example, with Sam, one could say,

> I see you have drawn a lot of moving vans crashing into cars, houses and people. . . . I guess you've moved a lot in your life and it's really upset you and left you feeling pretty hurt and angry.

or, at another time,

> I see the helicopter pilot is repairing the hole in the road. . . . I wonder if at times you feel that I'm like that pilot helping you mend some of your hurts.

At certain times this use of interpretation seems greatly to facilitate transference and growth. Its use becomes particularly important when a child becomes "stuck" in strong ambivalent feelings that he is unable to separate on his own. In these drawings, the positive images or symbols (babies, young children, flowers, trees) are constantly being destroyed by negative forces (explosions, guns, knives, logs, trucks). The repetition of an ambivalent theme over four to five sessions, coupled with the counselor's internal feeling ("this child is stuck"), is the stimulus for the counselor to reflect and interpret into the dynamics of the process. For example, if Billie kept on drawing "mean trees throwing spears at little Jack Pumpkinhead," the counselor could say something like:

> Billie, I've noticed this is the fourth time that the mean tree has tried to kill Jack. . . . I guess the tree is very angry at Jack and wants to hurt him. . . . Perhaps part of you is still really angry at your Mum for leaving home, and this anger "pops up" in you every now and again and makes you wreck things. What else

does the mean tree want to do? . . . I wonder if there's anything
we can do for the tree to make him feel better so he won't need to
continually hurt Jack.

In this way, it is possible to dialogue with the images of the
drawings and the child's outer reality at the same time. What is
occurring in the drawing symbolically represents an inner psychological struggle. Rapport, timing, and accuracy of the interpretation are key variables here if the child is to accept and understand
the interpretation. Resolution and behavior change can be initiated and invoked on a symbolic level—hence, the counselor's request to the tree. Here the counselor is acknowledging the angry
part of the child (as symbolized by the "mean tree") and offering to
help it.

In the termination stage, the counselor should emphasize the
positive aspects in the pictures, the ascendency of the hero figures,
and the order and calmness that have been restored. For example,
with Billie, on his last picture one could say:

> The grandmother really looks happy; she has lots of good food
> near her. . . . The dangerous log is losing its power. . . . You
> seem to be feeling so much better these days, and the teacher tells
> me you are enjoying school, making friends, and doing your
> work.

Another aspect of this stage is for the counselor to review the
child's progress with him:

> Remember when you first came in to see me, Billie: life was
> pretty hard for you, wasn't it? But by drawing with me about
> some of your thoughts and feelings you have changed a lot.

The counselor must leave the child with an awareness of how to
ask for help. Near the end the counselor could ask, "Billie, if
something upsets you in the future, what do you think you would
do about it?" Then the counselor works with this response until
the child has described a number of possible coping strategies. At

45

the very end, the counselor can lay out all of the pictures on the table or floor in chronological order and have the child review them ("What do you think of when you see all of your drawings?") and add some summative comments ("When you first came in I noticed you drew . . . and then . . . and now your drawings seem to show . . ."). The counselor then asks the child whether he or she wants the file with all the pictures or whether parents or counselor should keep them in a safe place for retrieval later.

Directive Approach

With the directive approach to serial drawing, the counselor suggests the topics and images for the child to draw until he or she starts to draw spontaneously or rejects the counselor's topics. Some children seem to need a little help and direction in order to start the process of drawing and self-disclosure. Once again timing is critical, because inevitably one reaches a point where it is no longer appropriate for the counselor to make a suggestion; that is, the child's own psychological drives are ready to take over. Simply stated, the directive method involves the counselor's asking the child to draw or re-draw a particular image or symbol that seems to match the child's emotional state or that seems to have symbolic relevance to the child.

There are three main components to this method: (a) use of the House–Tree–Person (H–T–P) test (Buck, 1948), (b) directed drawings, and (c) free drawings.

Use of the House–Tree–Person Test. Once rapport has been established, the counselor proceeds by administering the H–T–P test. After the three drawings have been completed, the counselor places the house drawing back in front of the child and proceeds with a simplified post-test inquiry. For each picture the counselor asks: (a) "Is there a story that goes with the picture?" (b) "Has anyone ever hurt the house?" (c) "What does the house need?" (d) "Does the house have a wish?" The counselor ends the session by saying, "I've asked you to draw three pictures for me and I wonder if you would like to do a drawing of your own choice now?" (If the child takes a long time over each drawing, spread them out over several sessions.) Based on these four drawings, the counselor assesses whether to intervene with directed images or free choice drawings.

Directed Drawings. Though there are many possible diagnostic indicators in the H–T–P test, it has been my observation that children reveal specific emotional concerns or needs by: (a) spending a considerable time on one particular aspect of the drawing, (b) focusing on a particular symbolic component (e.g., a flower, a light fixture, a bedroom, or a smoking chimney), or (c) experiencing a considerable affect from one image (e.g., black clouds, a broken tree, or an exploding bomb).

These three processes tend to reflect either a stuck emotional position (i.e., blocked affect) or an area where new psychological growth is possible. When using the directed drawing technique, the counselor focuses on either the painful area or the area of new growth and asks the child to draw another picture of that particular image. The counselor takes these drawings as meaningful representations of inner emotional states and, at the start of the next session, asks for further amplification. For example:

> I've been thinking about the drawings you did last week, and I remember that you spent a lot of time on the broken tree. I wonder how the tree is doing this week and whether you could draw me another picture of it.

When working with images and symbols, the counselor talks directly to the symbol as if it were real. In other words, the symbol is used as a focusing device or as a vehicle through which further growth can occur. When the counselor accurately focuses in on the key symbolic area, the child is usually willing to go ahead with additional drawings. If there are many symbols of pain, the counselor selects the one the child seems most involved in.

In the subsequent sessions, the counselor looks at the new drawings for symbols of either pain (hurt, wounds, damage) or growth (new trees, flowers, babies). In the early sessions, if indicated, the focus of the counselor's direction needs to be on the pain areas ("Could you draw me a close-up of the broken branch in last

47

week's picture?"), whereas once images of growth have ascendency in the pictures, the counselor follows that lead in the next session:

> I remember last week you drew the broken branch on the ground, and when that was finished you added flowers and a hummingbird. I wonder what's going on with them this week. Could you draw me a picture of the flowers and the birds?

Though this method is quite directive, it must be remembered that the counselor takes his or her sense of direction from the material the child produces.

Free Drawings. In the beginning phases, symbols of pain, emptiness or fixation frequently occur. But often, toward the end of the counseling sessions, the directed drawings reveal neither areas of pain nor areas of new growth. Then the counselor simply asks the child to do a drawing of his or her own choice.

A case study will illustrate the directive approach. It should be noted that throughout the counseling sessions no attempt was made to interpret the drawings to the child. Rather, the focus was placed on the content of the drawings (symbols) and on encouragement to explore the themes further.

Case Study

Dennis, a seven-year-old boy in second grade, was referred for counseling in September by his teacher because of his failure to adjust to the new class. He was very quiet, withdrawn, looked sad, had no friends, and was very anxious about attempting any new tasks. He became helpless whenever any work was required of him and usually tried to get another child to do it for him. His parents were in the process of a bitter divorce, and he had been placed by a judge in his grandmother's home.

Session One. Dennis was asked to draw the H–T–P series, and immediately his concern with the ground became apparent. His house was drawn with heavy bars over the three windows, and he spent ten minutes shading the ground under the house (fig. 2.21). The tree had a straight trunk with a few squiggly lines as bare branches near the top. Once again, the ground line was drawn and

FIG. 2.21   The house

a very elaborate root system depicted under the tree (fig. 2.22). In the post-test inquiry, he described the tree as "hurting because they tore its skin off." Later, he added, "The roots will help the tree get better."

Session Two. The focus in this session was placed on the underground and on the roots. This was done for two reasons: first, Dennis spent a long time drawing both the ground under the house and the root system of the tree; and second, he had indicated where the area of healing might occur by stating, "The roots will help the tree get better." At the start of this session, then, the counselor said:

> Dennis, I've been thinking about the hurt tree and the roots. I remembered what you said about them. It looks like the roots have a lot to offer the tree. I am wondering if you could do another picture of the roots for me.

49

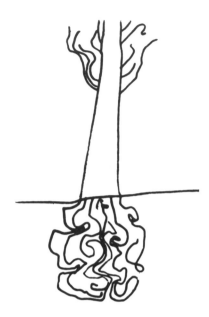

FIG. 2.22   The tree

Once again, Dennis was very involved in the drawing and drew a more elaborate root system but this time added in worms and their homes. He was very careful to ensure that each of the worms had its own home (fig. 2.23).

Session Three. Since a significant new area (worm homes) was revealed in the last session, the counselor asked Dennis to draw a picture of a worm's home and to show what goes on inside it. Dennis drew a mother worm in her home caring for the baby worms, some of whom had not yet hatched and were still in their eggs. He also drew a large spider that he said was food for the babies. There were ten worms and fourteen worm eggs. Each worm had eyes and a nose but no mouth. The mother was huge (at least twelve times as big) in comparison to the babies (fig. 2.24).

This drawing seemed to reflect the activation of the mother archetype (Neumann, 1974), psychological incubation (the eggs), nourishment (i.e., food), and rebirth (the babies). In other words, the transference to the counselor was beginning to activate the feel-

FIG. 2.23   Worm homes

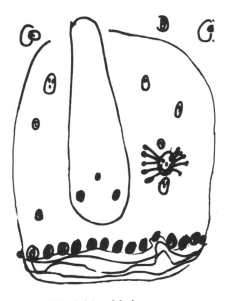

FIG. 2.24   Mother worm

ings of acceptance and caring which, in turn, generated new psychological life and growth in the child.

Session Four. It seemed that the mother worm and the babies were the key features in the previous drawing, so the counselor asked Dennis to draw the mother worm and one of her babies. His picture showed the very large mother worm, with a big smile and more human facial features, beaming down on a just-hatched baby worm who is surrounded by hearts. The scene depicts an exchange of love between the mother and child. Dennis wrote the words "I love you" near the mother worm, with the baby worm replying, "I love you too" (fig. 2.25).

Session Five. As the previous picture seemed to reflect the start of the internalization of a positive mother–infant attachment, the counselor pursued this issue further by asking Dennis to draw another scene of the mother worm and her son. This drawing showed that the baby worm had grown four times its original size and was now a "child" worm. The mother says to the child worm,

FIG. 2.25   "I love you"

"Can you help me?" and he answers "O.K." The mother then tells the child, "You are good," and the child replies, "You are good, too" (fig. 2.26).

Session Six. As certain critical aspects seemed resolved and as the previous drawing did not seem to indicate a definite direction, the counselor said to Dennis, "I've asked you to draw several pictures, and today I'm wondering if there is anything you would like to draw."

His picture showed on the left-hand side a boy smiling in the bright sunshine saying, "I am happy." At the right side of the drawing, clouds, rain, and lightning were present but did not impinge on the boy (fig. 2.27). The drawing seemed to reflect that the stormy period of his life was moving away and was being replaced by more positive and happy feelings. The turmoil was still there at the edge of his life, but it was not dominating all of his existence. The teacher at this point commented on the child's dramatic overall improvement. His happiness showed on his face

FIG. 2.26   Boy worm

FIG. 2.27   I am happy

and, in class, he was making friends and doing much more work on his own. Not only that, he was becoming more daring and even disobeying the teacher at times.

Session Seven. In order to focus once again on the positive aspects and to help internalize them, the counselor asked Dennis to draw a picture of "the boy in the sunshine." This drawing showed a happy, smiling boy in the sun with no signs of a storm. Dennis wrote next to the boy, "I am happy and I am glad because the rain has gone away" (fig. 2.28).

Sessions Eight, Nine, Ten. Dennis's drawings began to change at this point, and he drew pictures of many situations with his friends. At the start of the ninth session, the counselor announced the termination procedures and Dennis drew a spaceman getting ready for blast-off to the moon. The story that went with it was expansive and positive.

Contact with the teacher and grandmother, with whom he was living, now indicated that he was out of his shell, his academic

away
The ran has gon
I am glad. becus
I am hape and

FIG. 2.28   Boy in the sunshine

work was improving, and he was able to concentrate on his school work. Also, his behavior had improved; he was making friends and moving into neighborhood activities.

Follow-up. A follow-up session was held five months later, and Dennis was asked to do four drawings: H–T–P and an underground scene. All the pictures reflected healthy images. The house was open at the front, and one could see people eating at a table under the lights (fig. 2.29); the tree was the normal trunk and leafy top of the primary-aged child (fig. 2.30); and the person was his friend, the next-door-neighbor child. When asked to draw a picture of the ground underneath the earth, he reacted with surprise and seemed to have no recollection of drawing the series of underground pictures some months before. The new drawing had no resemblance to the previous ones and showed a busy, interesting place filled with life and activity. There was a good connection between the outside world and the underground through a system of tunnels and roots. Unlike the earlier drawing of the bar-

FIG. 2.29   Home

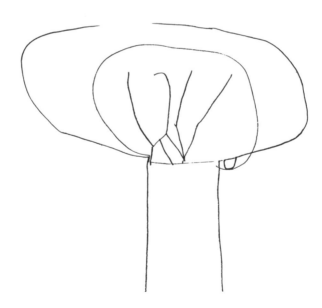

FIG. 2.30   Tree

ren tree, the plants appeared healthy both above and below the ground. There were ants, worms, buried money, old and new cents, and even a miner going down one tunnel to find the "lost treasure" (fig. 2.31). This drawing seemed to reflect continued psychological growth and the establishment of a positive relationship between his conscious and unconscious mind (i.e., easy access to the underground and many positive symbols). Follow-up, three years after the termination of treatment, indicated no problems and continued development.

Partially Directed Approach

In this method of serial drawing, the counselor identifies a visual theme that has relevance to the child, and every four to six weeks asks the child to draw that image. In the intervening sessions, the child is free to draw whatever he or she wishes. These partially directed drawings are often useful indicators of the progress that

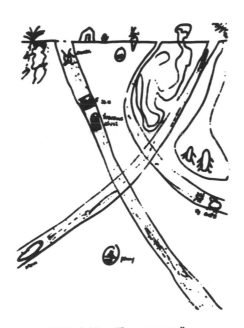

FIG. 2.31   "Lost treasure"

the child is making in treatment and can also offer a focal point for the psychological working through of a particular symbolic issue that the child is struggling with.

At the start of treatment, in the assessment phase, the child is asked to do an H–T–P series followed by a picture of his own choice. Following the post-test inquiry and a discussion (from the child's frame of reference) of the child's free drawing, the counselor assesses which picture carries the most symbolic meaning for the child. Usually one image or symbol seems to stand out. The image alone may not look meaningful, but when the child describes the image, the intensity of meaning becomes apparent. For some children it is the house, some the tree, some the person, while for others this specific intense meaning appears in their free drawing. It may be anything: a butterfly, a river, a horse, a battlefield, a car, or a dog. The counselor makes an assessment, keeps the image in mind, allows the therapy to progress as the child wishes, but when another assessment or review is needed, the child may be asked to draw the specific image identified earlier. The case below describes one way to use this approach and the results.

Case Background

Carl, a sixth grader who lost his temper if things were not "perfect," was referred to the school counselor because of acting out behaviors and alienation from friends. Although an excellent student, he often created problems through his own anxiety. His family were just going through a divorce, and Carl alternated between being either explosive or withdrawn.

He talked freely in the first session, said he got into trouble a lot, did not like it but was not sure why it happened. He did an H–T–P, wanted a ruler, and asked, "Do you want me to do it [the house] looking down?" He spent twenty minutes on the house, meticulously drawing the front door and stained glass windows, four minutes on the tree, and about six minutes on the person, a hockey goalie. During the post-test inquiry, he focused more on the tree, adding the wind ("it's slanting because the wind is blowing") and the fungus ("the tree is growing fungus on it") (fig. 2.32).

FIG. 2.32   Fungus tree

During the next four sessions, Carl drew self-portraits and talked about life at school. He did some role-playing about being cooperative and non-cooperative and identified feelings connected with each role. At home he was often in tears and refused to talk about the separation. At the start of the sixth session, the counselor said:

> Carl, I've been thinking about the windstorm and the tree. I wonder what has happened to the tree, the growth on the trunk and its condition.

Carl immediately started to draw the tree, saying "It's got more rotten." He then colored it, adding "Wood bugs and ants are eating away inside where it is rotten" (fig. 2.33).

Over the following three sessions, Carl continued to talk about school and was able to acknowledge that his parents were splitting

FIG. 2.33 Wood bugs and ants

up, though he added, "It doesn't really bother me." Life in school continued to improve, and after another month the counselor stated at the start of a session, "Carl, I wonder how the tree is doing?" He immediately replied, "It's fallen down" and proceeded to draw it lying on the ground with grass sprouting from it. Later he commented, "There are bugs and ants in the log still" (fig. 2.34).

In the next few sessions, he began to talk openly about the divorce and his hurt, sad and mad feelings. The counselor tied together his feelings about the divorce and getting into trouble. He said at times he tried to pretend the divorce was not happening but then would get really mad when he knew it was. He was having a few more eruptions at school and was feeling embarrassed and mad at himself. He started to cry and to talk about how his life used to be fun and went smoothly. But now things had changed and would never be the same. He was acutely experiencing the pain over the divorce and the loss of father and family. Toward the

FIG. 2.34   It's fallen down

end of the session the counselor asked, "I wonder how the tree is doing?" Carl started to draw it and said, "It's decaying" (fig. 2.35).

In the next five sessions Carl talked about life at school, his father, and issues that bothered him. With problem-solving and role-playing, he approached various conflicts. He had a violent outburst at school, damaged some property, and felt very embarrassed and upset. It was a big step for him to be able to talk about his part in it, to accept the fact that he had blown it, and to apologize to the teacher. When this was worked through, the counselor asked him how the tree was doing. He replied, "The tree has decayed into dirt and there's new bushes" (fig. 2.36). There were a few more sessions up to the end of the school year in which Carl was able to talk quite freely about his struggles, and counseling was terminated at this point. He called his last picture "The New Tree" (fig. 2.37).

Follow-up a year and eight months later with Carl, now an

eighth grader, indicated a well-adjusted boy. When asked about the tree he said, "It's developed into a new one. It's a strong tree now, and there's a waterfall flowing down the hillside beside it" (fig. 2.38).

This whole sequence of tree drawing seems to reflect the process of psychological death and re-birth. The counselor felt that Carl had let go of his childhood, experienced the pain of divorce, and was now on his way to becoming a confident young adolescent. The hurt had been expressed and shared, the wounds healed, and new growth was now possible.

FIG. 2.35   It's decaying

FIG. 2.36   New bushes

FIG. 2.37   New tree

FIG. 2.38   Strong tree

Chapter 3

SPONTANEOUS AND DIRECTED DRAWINGS WITH SEXUALLY AND PHYSICALLY ABUSED CHILDREN

SEXUAL AND PHYSICAL acts of abuse result in deep physical and psychical scars: sensations, images and emotions are internalized by the child, and part of the child's psychological development becomes stuck. But in my experience, just talking about these acts is insufficient to resolve the trauma. Painting, drawing, making (in clay) and play enactment are very helpful ways of externalizing these forms of abuse and hence enabling the psyche to be healed and move forward.

Sexual Abuse

Just how devastating sexual abuse is on psychological life can be seen in the following pictures. Figure 3.1 shows the drawing of a thirteen-year-old boy a few days prior to his being anally raped. Following this experience, the boy was hospitalized for a psychotic episode. During the early part of treatment, he drew three pictures (figs. 3.2, 3.3, 3.4) which show perceptual distortions, re-enactment of sexual trauma, and regressions to oral and anal stages of development. Drawings of another boy who was also hospitalized for psychosis—after witnessing his father rape his sixteen-year-old sister and mother—depicted obsessive-compulsive ruminations, identity confusions, the mechanization of flesh and body parts, death, blood, bones, and implements of torture. The father was drawn in the center of the picture as a small king with a war axe for his penis. Stewart (1987) observed that sexual violation of the incest taboo often produces a reaction of psychotic intensity.

Petra was seven years old and in the second grade when she was

FIG. 3.1   St. George

FIG. 3.2   Banish the witch

your hands

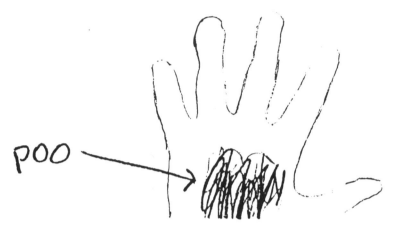

poo

FIG. 3.3   Poo on your hand

new Brau

FIG. 3.4   New brau

referred for counseling by her classroom teacher. She had just been returned to her home school after spending one school year in a special class. Petra was having extreme difficulty adjusting to the classroom, was uncontrollable and acted in a borderline psychotic way: at times violent, then withdrawn, incoherent and mentioning bizarre fantasies. The counselor, one of my graduate students, became, for her, the one adult in the school with whom she could interact on a one-to-one basis.

Because Petra's English was limited at this time (English was her second language), she was fairly non-verbal. The counselor used drawing as a way to help her express her thoughts and feelings. At first, the subjects were of her own choice, but later in the sessions together, as critical issues began to appear, the counselor suggested a topic for the drawings and Petra readily followed the suggestion. In fact, she seemed relieved when the drawings were directed, as if the directions took her to an area of pain that she wanted to disclose and share. This process seemed to deepen her trust and greatly facilitated the counseling.

At first the counselor simply said to her: "You might like to draw as we talk." She immediately picked up the felt pen and began scribbling and talking: "It's a dream. . . . No, it's a nightmare. I dreamt my Daddy got into bed with me" (fig. 3.5). Because this girl was having intense psychotic-like reactions, we (her counselor and I) began to suspect sexual abuse. As she was unable to talk and as much of her pain centered around her home, we started the next session by asking her to complete the House-Tree-Person test (Buck, 1948) and to Draw-the-Family. She drew herself in a very light, sketchy way (fig. 3.6) and both the house and her family in a violent way with scribbling all over (figs. 3.7 and 3.8). The most revealing picture was the tree (fig. 3.9) which looked like an erect phallus. Petra said, "The wind is blowing so strongly that the birds are flying backward. . . . The tree is dead because they chopped it down. It needs food and love." The case was reported to the Provincial Sexual Abuse Team.

As Petra's treatment continued the pictures became more distinct and graphic. There were many bedroom and bathroom

FIG. 3.5   It's a nightmare

FIG. 3.6   Me

FIG. 3.7   My house

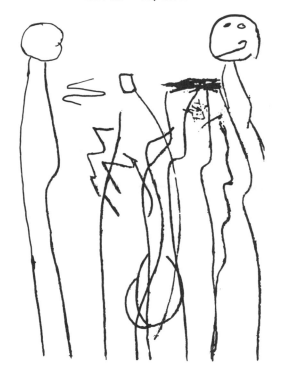

FIG. 3.8   My family

FIG. 3.9   The tree is dead

scenes (fig. 3.10) and drawings of people on top of each other (fig. 3.11). In her Draw-the-Family, all the males were drawn with their genitals (fig. 3.12). Once these experiences had been portrayed on paper, she moved on to other topics. Never once did she talk about what had happened, and when the counselor tried to bring it up Petra started to talk about something else.

Art counseling not only formed the main part of treatment, but also helped Petra express and draw her wishes (Silver, 1978). To a certain extent, some of the feeling she was not getting from the "real" world could be provided in and through her drawings, which showed some of the critical issues facing her then. She drew pictures of herself roller-skating with her friends, though in actual fact she had no friends. She drew pictures of her mother spending time talking to her, but we knew from interviews with the family that this was not happening.

In the second year of treatment she often drew her classroom teacher (a male who gave her a lot of attention) as her father and

FIG. 3.10   Bathrooms

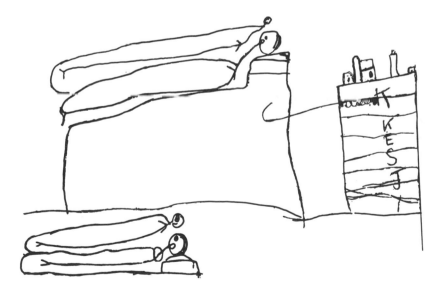

FIG. 3.11   Bedrooms

FIG. 3.12   My family

through the drawing gained some of the positive feelings about herself (fig. 3.13), and about healthy affection with a male, that her own father did not give her. Drawing these "wishes" partially satisfied her need to feel loved and wanted and seemed to help her internalize positive affects.

The counselor worked with Petra in weekly one-to-one sessions for two school years, and her psychological growth during this time was remarkable. Her last picture, in color, showed herself as a princess (fig. 3.14). She is presently enrolled in a regular eighth-grade class and is showing no signs of the early behavior that led her first to a special class and then to individual counseling sessions. For Petra and for children like her, a combination of free and directed art counseling is a powerful tool for change.

FIG. 3.13   My teacher George

FIG. 3.14   A princess

Physical Abuse

Colin was twelve when he was referred to a child guidance clinic for treatment of violent and destructive behavior. He had kicked his nine-year-old sister, and she died a few days later of a ruptured spleen. The background indicated a history of chronic physical abuse by an alcoholic father for at least nine years. Colin was very extroverted and liked to talk about horror movies and rock bands and draw in his spare time. Rapport was easily established in the first session (fig. 3.15), and as "homework" he was encouraged to draw outside of the sessions. He brought his drawings in, and we started each session talking about them.

His early pictures revealed, both graphically and by written word, his deep guilt and shame over his sister's death and his anger and fear of males in positions of authority (figs. 3.16 and 3.17). Following this, he did a series of drawings about what his father

FIG. 3.15   My friend

FIG. 3.16   Prison guards

FIG. 3.17   Teacher

did to him (figs. 3.18 and 3.19). These showed his father whipping him, hitting him in the face, kicking him in the stomach, throwing him on the floor. Discussion of the drawings led to how he felt when hit and later to an understanding of why his dad acted this way.

As the therapy progressed, Colin brought in a series of drawings about space travel and other adventures (figs. 3.20 and 3.21). Invariably, the male therapist was included in the drawings as a hero who would die on a hostile planet (figs. 3.22 and 3.23). An interpretation was made about how hopeless Colin must feel about himself and about the therapist's ability to help him. Colin became very depressed and in one session brought in a picture of himself in hell, never dying and being forced to "see forever my sister's body" (fig. 3.24). We spent a long time on this theme, but after some months of continued work there was a resolution. He said one day, "you know, my sister was sent to me like a message. This happened so I would get help."

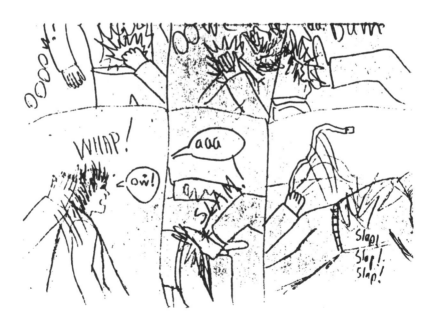

FIG. 3.18   WHAP

FIG. 3.19   SLAM

FIG. 3.20   Spaceship list

FIG. 3.21   Hostile planet

FIG. 3.22   Eaten alive

FIG. 3.23   Death

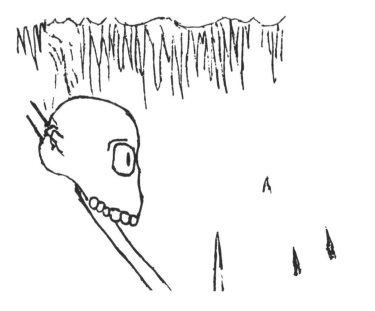

FIG. 3.24   Hell

More work needed to be done regarding the father. An understanding of Colin's relationship with his father came through a terrifying dream and following amplification by drawing. Colin dreamt that a bound monster emerged from a swamp (fig. 3.25), strode over to a man and picked him up by his neck (fig. 3.26). However, he did not kill him but put him down and turned to face Colin (fig. 3.27). Colin screamed in the dream when the man looked at him because he realized it was himself. In talking about this Colin said, "This man is me. In the dream I wanted to strangle my father for his abuse of me but I didn't. When the monster turned to look at me I was scared shitless. You know I wanted revenge. I wanted to hurt him. But I won't. I feel safer now with my anger. It's in me but I don't need to do it. My Dad has problems and needs help."

Soon after this, Colin was discharged from residential treatment, returned to school, and eight years later graduated from college. He is now married and working successfully as a graphic artist.

FIG. 3.25   Bound monster

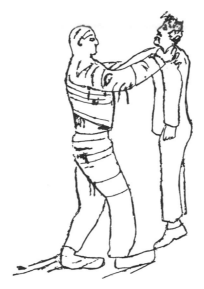

FIG. 3.26   Lifts him up

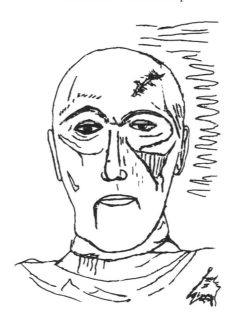

FIG. 3.27   Myself

Chapter 4

THE ROSEBUSH:
A VISUALIZATION STRATEGY FOR IDENTIFICATION
OF POSSIBLE CHILD ABUSE

THERE SEEMS TO have been an increase in the past few years in the use of art, drawing, visualization, and imagery in children's counseling (Allan, 1978; Allan and Clark, 1984; Anderson, 1980; Fino, 1978; Pinholster, 1983; Roosa, 1981; Wittmer and Myrick, 1980). Although there had been many critical evaluations of these methods (Bellak, 1954; Gamna and Bortino, 1980; Harrower, 1954; Korner, 1956; Rabin, 1981; Singer, 1981), practicing school counselors find them useful in their work with students.

In this particular study we compared the visual imagery (i.e., the drawings) and the metaphorical statements (i.e., the words used to describe the pictures) of coping and non-coping children. The purpose was to determine whether the pictures and words of the coping children reflect emotional health, whereas those of non-coping children signify inner turmoil.

A coping child was simply defined as one who gets along well with the teacher and peers and shows average developmental mastery of learning skills. Non-coping was defined as the converse: failure to get along with teacher and peers and failure to master the work skills necessary at the child's grade level. A trained and experienced elementary school counselor in an urban school district was asked to help a group of teachers identify 10 coping and 10 non-coping children from a group of 120 fourth and fifth graders. Students were selected for the study if they fell into the average IQ range on the Wechsler Intelligence Scale for Children—Revised (Wechsler, 1974) and were from similar socioeconomic backgrounds.

Procedure

The treatment consisted of three phases—relaxation and imagery, drawing, and postdrawing inquiry—and was conducted by one researcher (a graduate student from the university). Each child was seen separately for about one hour.

Relaxation and Imagery. A ten-minute audiotape on relaxation and guided visualization was developed, based on the imagery of a rosebush (Oaklander, 1978; Stevens, 1971). It was assumed that the students would project various facets of their personalities into the image of the rosebush. The tape was introduced to the children as a way to develop the imagination. A first section on relaxation was followed by a suggestion that they visualize themselves as a rosebush, noting their flowers, leaves, stems, and branches (see Appendix A).

Drawing. After a relaxation and imagery activity, the children were presented with a piece of white, 8½-by-11-inch paper, a pencil, and a set of twelve colored crayons and were asked to draw a picture of what they imagined during the guided visualization.

Postdrawing Inquiry. After the drawing, the researcher asked the children eleven questions about their experience as a rosebush, such as, "What do you look like? Tell me about your flowers, your leaves, your roots. Who takes care of you?" (See Appendix B.)

All responses were taped for subsequent transcription and evaluation. The researcher noted the children's behavior during the procedure, including the place on the paper where they started the drawing. Each child was given a code number, and the researcher did not know whether the children were identified as coping or non-coping.

Data Analysis

The information collected on each child was evaluated in three ways: sorting, picture analysis, and statement analysis.

Sorting. Three school counselors, trained in testing and projective techniques, were asked to sort the material into two piles (copers and non-copers) in three different ways: when given the drawings alone, when given only the child's first statements about the rosebush, and when given the child's drawing and first statements together.

Picture Analysis. The drawings were analyzed by contrasting pairs of positive and negative characteristics, as developed by Elkisch (1960). These characteristics were: rhythm versus rule, complexity versus simplexity, expansion versus compression, and integration versus disintegration.

"Rhythm" involves flexible strokes that show a free, relaxed movement with a pleasingly proportional distribution of an object; "rule" indicates a tight, spasmodic movement often done mechanically. "Complexity" refers to a complete or detailed drawing, while "simplexity" is a lack of detail and impoverished differentiation that suggests regression or fixation in earlier stages of development. "Expansion" reflects a sense of spaciousness in the drawing, whereas "compression" gives the feeling of meticulous smallness or the experience of being squeezed in. "Integration" provides a feeling of the whole with things in place, demonstrating an ability to relate, combine, and organize; "disintegration" represents sloppiness and the use of unrelated and disconnected objects, so that a sense of oneness is not evoked.

Statement Analysis. After gathering all responses to the post-drawing questions about the rosebush, the researcher made descriptive comparisons between the statements of the copers and non-copers. The statements were sorted into positive, neutral, and negative phrases.

Results

The general descriptions here are based on the researcher's observations during the interview, the drawing activity, and the postdrawing inquiry.

Approach to Drawing. Of the twenty children, nineteen approached the activity without hesitation and started to draw right away. Both copers and non-copers seemed concerned with doing a good job, carefully choosing colors, and concentrating on the task at hand. One child, a non-coper, was detached, aloof, and disinterested in the activities.

Initial Placement. Of the ten copers, eight started their picture in the middle of the page; seven non-copers started at the bottom.

Rosebush Perspective. The size of the rosebush in relation to the rest of the picture did not seem to differentiate between the two groups. Six copers positioned the rosebush in proper perspective, one drew it very small, and three drew it very large. Four non-copers used a proper perspective, but three made very large and three made very small drawings. These findings challenge Bolander's (1977) assumption that healthy, well-adjusted children would put the central figure in the appropriate perspective.

Color Analysis. Both groups used color in their drawings, and neither group used an excess of any particular color. Two children (one coper and one non-coper) did not color their pictures.

Analysis by Raters

When placing the children into coper and non-coper categories on the basis of drawings only, the three raters agreed on sixteen cases out of twenty $(p < .05)$. When they sorted the two categories based on the children's first statements about the rosebush (i.e., without the picture), there was agreement on only twelve cases out of twenty $(p > .05)$. When pictures and statements were combined and presented to the raters, there was agreement in sorting eighteen out of twenty cases $(p < .01)$.

These findings suggest that the "picture only" category in the eyes of experienced counselors yielded significant discrimination. The "picture and statement" category gave added influence and was more significant than the "picture only" pile.

Two students in the coping group were consistently placed in the non-coping group by the raters, and two non-coping students were always placed in the coping group. Such placements could indicate that twenty percent of the time teachers and counselors miss the pain in the coping child and the strengths in the non-coping child.

Analysis of Elkisch Categories

Elkisch (1960) claimed that the four categories described earlier could be used to distinguish between coping and non-coping children. In this sample of twenty children, we found that only the categories of rhythm versus rule ($p < .01$) and integration versus disintegration ($p < .05$) differentiated between the two groups. In this case, non-copers showed more signs of rule (rigidity) and disintegration (sloppiness) than did coping children.

Analysis of Children's Statements

The children's responses to stimulus questions about the rosebush were transcribed, and a comparison was made between the descriptive imagery used by copers and non-copers. Differences between copers and non-copers were consistently found in descriptions of the rosebush, flowers, thorns, environments, and caretakers, but not in descriptions of stems, branches, leaves, roots, and the climate (see table 1).

TABLE 1

Children's Descriptions of the Rosebush

Attributes of the Rosebush	Copers	Non-copers
Rosebush	I'm pretty. My flowers are colorful. I'm blooming. I'm friendly and strong.	I'm very mean. I'm sad. I'm fat. I don't feel good.
Flowers	The flower is velvety. They feel soft and silky.	No flowers 'coz someone moved away and took them. When you try to pick one they hurt.
Thorns	I protect myself with them. They are small. They keep me safe.	They are very sharp and mean. They draw blood. There's poison in them.
Environment	I live in a field. I've got grass and Mother Nature. It's colorful here. Big trees and blue sky.	I'm in the middle of a desert. Behind a picket fence in a parking lot. I see broken bottles and glass.

| Caretakers | The mother—I like it.
The dad and children.
Mother Nature.
The people and things around
me. | Nobody takes care of me.
I can't feed or water myself.
There used to be a gatekeeper but
he had a heart attack.
I look after myself because people
bug me and cut me down. |

As can be seen from table 1, copers projected a strong self-image, positive associations attached to touching experiences, an ability to protect themselves, and a tendency to see their environment as pleasant and as containing friendly caretakers. In contrast, non-copers used words to describe negative self-concepts, painful associations to touching experiences, and an extremely aggressive, hostile environment with destructive caretakers.

Analysis of Specific Protocols

At the termination of the project, the elementary school counselor who had selected the coping and non-coping children informed us that, in the non-coping group, five children had been sexually abused, one physically abused, and one severely neglected. We decided to examine the protocols (i.e., both the drawings and the descriptive comments about the drawings) of these children in greater detail. For comparison, we have also included below the protocol of a child from the coping sample.

Coping children tended to draw pictures with very positive images: the rosebush was blooming, the sun was out, and the positive aspects of nature were always present. For example, a coping child drew a rosebush full of flowers, with a mother bird flying toward it with a worm in her mouth for the babies nesting there. Small trees and a rabbit line the bottom border of the drawing (fig. 4.1).

On the other hand, the sexually abused children's drawings and statements seemed to reveal three themes: (a) sexual imagery —"There's a lot of caterpillar eggs on the leaves," "A bee came along and took some of the stuff out of it"; (b) a violation of the core self—"The dog is going to lick the flower, the hand is going to grab the flower, the flower does not want to be touched"; and (c) protection—many of the rosebushes had fences all the way

FIG. 4.1   Coping child

around them and children stated such things as "A woodman came down and tried to cut me down but I wouldn't let him." These children's pictures often reflected damage to the core symbol and protection of it by strong fences (figs. 4.2, 4.3 and 4.4). A girl who had been anally raped drew the rosebush in figure 4.5.

Unlike sexually abused children, the physically abused child drew a picture that reflected evidence of severe physical violence. For example, one child drew a cracked, ruptured road, leading to a house with smashed windows and barred doorways. Even though the rosebush (with very pronounced thorns) was placed in the foreground of the picture, it was tiny in comparison to the other themes in the picture (fig. 4.6).

The rosebush of the neglected child was the only one in all the pictures to be cut off from the ground. It was placed in a glass with little water in the middle of the paper. No other themes existed so that the picture gave a sense of impoverishment and barrenness (fig. 4.7).

FIG. 4.2   Non-coping: Sexually abused

FIG. 4.3   Non-coping: Sexually abused

FIG. 4.4   Non-coping: Sexually abused: Rosebush covered by fence

FIG. 4.5   Non-coping: Anally raped

FIG. 4.6   Non-coping: Physically abused

Conclusions

The results of this study indicated that counselors trained in projective techniques can differentiate eighty percent of the time between coping and non-coping children through drawings and statements. Furthermore, the pictures of non-copers showed more signs of disintegration and rigidity than did those of copers. Most copers started their pictures in the middle of the page, whereas non-copers started at the bottom of the page.

Children's drawings and the words they use to describe them can give the school counselor a view into their inner world of feelings. A counselor trained in the use of projective techniques and in understanding the emotions embedded in metaphorical language can identify students who might need some individual attention. In working with children's drawings, counselors need to help children verbalize their thoughts and feelings about the contents of the

FIG. 4.7   Non-coping: Emotionally neglected

pictures. This can be done by asking the child to talk from the perspective of the image used (e.g., from one rosebush's point of view). The image provides a safe vehicle for children to project some of their own thoughts and feelings, paving the way to talk more directly later about them (Allan, 1978; Allan and Clark, 1984).

For counselors, the rosebush strategy may be a useful screening device for detecting children who have been or are being sexually abused. The rosebush seems to symbolize an emotional essence of the child; in this sample, those whose essences had been violated drew protective fences completely around the rosebush and used language indicative of sexual abuse or violation. Projective techniques, although often yielding useful information, must be used with great caution, and counselors interested in these approaches should receive or seek out some specialized and supervised training.

Counselors also can use the rosebush visualization and drawing activity as part of a group guidance activity. Later, the students can share their drawings, or the counselor can spend a few minutes with each child.

Chapter 5

SPONTANEOUS DRAWINGS
IN COUNSELING
SERIOUSLY ILL CHILDREN

EVERY LIFE MUST end in death. Every person deals with this inevitability in an individual way: some choose to ignore it; others dwell on it for years; most fear it. Those who become aware that their time is limited because of a terminal illness have an opportunity to work through a range of emotional responses to this ending. Such work often enables them to live each day more fully in spite of the emotional turmoil.

Children also are aware of life's ending. When the shortened life is that of a critically ill child or one much loved by a child, little emotion may be expressed in words, but a great deal might appear in symbolic form or in unusual behaviors. Teachers and counselors can be of value to such a child by supporting her or him through this difficulty (Bertoia and Allan, 1988). Parents and other related adults often are working through their own grief and are not able to meet the child's needs. The counselor can help by providing an opportunity for expressing these deep emotions through art. A skilled counselor can use interpretation to be of greater assistance, but even a novice in art counseling can set up opportunities for symbolic release through just the drawing process. Simply seeing the art the child produces often gives the counselor insight into what he or she is experiencing.

While there is abundant literature on children's cognitive understanding of death, we are focusing here on the child's self-concept and unconscious understanding of the dying process as revealed through his or her art.

Self-Concept

Much work has been done with terminally ill children which helps us to understand what is occurring in their worlds. Kubler-Ross (1983) found that children do know what is happening to them when they are dying. She indicates that the common grieving stages children experience are similar to those of adults: denial, anger, bargaining, depression, and acceptance. Acceptance in this case refers to an awareness of the situation and a determination to live fully in those days which are left. These stages may occur in any order, and some may be skipped. Some individuals may function primarily in one emotional stage through most of the dying process. Hope is often present: at some times hope for cure, at other times hope for unfinished business to be completed before death. Generalized fear will also be part of a child's experience.

In thousands of cases Kubler-Ross found that, through creative work, either written or drawn, children are at some inner level attuned to events in their lives and express this knowledge, often symbolically, to those who will hear them. She encourages those who work with critically ill or bereaved children to provide them with many opportunities for writing or drawing.

Bluebond-Langner (1978) studied the hospital stays of critically ill children. She found that children work through a continuum of self-concept phases: from being well to Stage 1 (seriously ill), to Stage 2 (seriously ill and will get better), to Stage 3 (always ill but will get better), to Stage 4 (always ill and will never get better), to Stage 5 (dying). This awareness is sequential. Specific events must be integrated with past information before the child moves to the next phase. No new phase is entered unless a child is in the previous stage when the precipitating event happens. Thus, even if a friend dies of the same disease, the child would not move into Stage 5 unless that news came in Stage 4.

It would seem possible that the stages identified by Kubler-Ross could easily be integrated with this changing self-concept schema. As the children arrive at each new phase of awareness, they would likely react again with denial, anger, and so forth. If the counselor can then be aware of process and allow the emotions to be experienced and vented in drawings with acceptance and understanding, the child can progress and will probably experience some sense of resolution and acceptance.

Spontaneous Drawings

A pioneer in the use of spontaneous drawings with dying children is the London Jungian psychotherapist Susan Bach (1966). Bach saw spontaneous drawings as reflecting the child's inner or psychological world and noticed that the drawings also revealed physiological information drawn by the child from the unconscious level of existence (i.e., the drawings reflected both the psychological state of the child and the somatic condition). Kiepenheuer (1980) also recognized the organic as well as psychological information appearing in patient drawings. These researchers' physiological diagnoses were later confirmed by the other medical specialists working with these children. Bach (1975) argues that someone trained in correctly reading the drawings gains information for helping the whole child.

Theoretical Assumptions. Before being able to understand the material shared in a drawing, the counselor must accept three postulates (Williams and Furth, 1985):

1.   There is an unconscious psyche, and it can express itself through spontaneous or impromptu drawings.

2.   Though the spontaneous or impromptu picture is an "uncommon" means of communication, it is valid and has meaning.

3.   The mind and body ("psyche" and "soma") are linked. This linkage allows for continuous communication between the two.

Assessing the Picture. Mastering the ability accurately to read a drawing will be challenging. Caution is needed, especially considering the risk of projecting one's own emotions and symbolism into another's drawing (Thompson and Allan, 1987). From a Jungian perspective, the symbol or image used in a picture is a container of feelings or emotions (Allan, 1978; Allan and Clark, 1984; Allan and Crandall, 1986). In looking at a picture the counselor silently asks, "What is the feeling tone of this image? What emotions is the child expressing here?" This gives the counselor an understanding of the child's inner emotional struggles. These struggles are often experienced first on an imagistic level before they reach verbal consciousness.

For those working with children and their art, Bach (1966) and Furth (1981) provide guidelines for "seeing" what is in the picture. Initially, one would spend time doing an inventory of what is in the picture and what is missing. Asking what is odd or what stands out in the picture helps focus on where the main psychic energy is. One records the choice of color, the lack of it, or its inappropriate use. As well, one notes and counts repeated occurrences, as the repetition is likely significant. Placement on the page and the relationship among the objects should be studied to understand what is in the foreground or background of the child's life. The child is the entire picture, but he or she also may identify with one object or person within it.

However, Allan (1978), Bach (1975), Kiepenheuer (1980), and Furth (1981) agree that the process of creative expression alone, in the presence of the counselor with no interpretation, will help children release some of the power of symbols and emotions at a critical time in their lives. Children can also work through the psychological process of serious illness and dying in this way. Simply being with the child and talking about the content of the picture in the third person ("I notice you've drawn a big gorilla; I wondered what the gorilla is thinking . . . feeling . . . and planning to do next") can help alleviate some of the loneliness and isolation that such children feel.

Helping the Family. The drawings are also a way that the child can communicate with the family what he or she is experiencing, and sharing this information with the family may help them in understanding the child's awareness and needs (Bach, 1975). The child can then communicate more effectively with them in the time remaining. For example, though children often find it hard to talk about their fears, they will tend to portray them quite visibly in the drawings. The drawing can then be used as a bridge for discussion and can also be shown to the parents to help them understand some of the child's inner struggles. If a resolution has been successfully achieved, the family will also gain comfort from the pictures and from knowing the child has reached a sense of peace (Furth, 1981). Even if resolution has not occurred, the parents and siblings have concrete images and pictures from the child's life.

Method

Each child is seen alone, and at the outset of each session after the initial rapport has been established, the child is asked what he or she would like to draw. If the child is visibly low in energy, the session is shortened or he is asked what he wants to do next, so that he always has some control and the choice of art is left open. Initially, children might need some reassurance that their drawings are really wanted, that they don't have to produce a "correct" piece of art as some art teachers might require.

The approaches used can vary. Some pictures can be spontaneous with no specific stimulus; others may be directed, such as, "Can you draw me a picture from one of your dreams?" Others are concrete representations of guided imagery activities. For children in a crisis situation, using relaxation techniques or guided imagery prior to drawing helps release both stress and the creativity of the unconscious. The children choose from oil pastels, crayons, felts, pencil crayons, or pencil. There will be times when they want to draw only abstracts and times when they might not want to draw at all.

When the child indicates the picture is complete, thank him or her, acknowledging the effort in some form also, date it, and ask if it has a title. Sometimes there is one, although often children do not have any. Sometimes there is a story to the picture and sometimes not. The child should dictate the story to the counselor, for the physical process of writing it out himself is too draining. If there is no story, talk about the picture a little. Sometimes the children will chat as they work but usually not. Again, follow each child's lead. Together the counselor and child place the newest addition to the art collection into a special folder. The process of setting up and filing become part of an established procedure or ritual, supporting the concept that counseling is a special time and that these are special and significant pictures.

Case Study

Caroyl was diagnosed while a first grader as having a terminal form of leukemia and received chemotherapy. Although she attended second grade at school when possible, she had been registered with the homebound counseling program during the summer to start third grade at home in September. For the first few months of her homebound program, she was in remission and at first glance did not appear very sick although she was always on medication.

It happened that the projects Caroyl chose to complete in her Language Arts school work included drawings. Her family was very pleased with her illustrated book of poems for Christmas. By January she was not as interested in the writing process (which included revisions on some pieces) but did enjoy doing illustrations, and as her health deteriorated our focus moved more to drawing. The artwork was taken as a story only, and no interpretation of the material or ownership of the emotions was done at that time, although discussions of the picture content in the third person became more frequent.

Her change in interest from dictating a story to only drawing was not a lack of keenness for school. Her two favorite activities were "do a drawing, and math." Even when she felt so ill she could not complete the regular schedule of subjects, the act of drawing provided enough release that her first love, math, could be managed.

At one point, when the counselor, Judi, was particularly distressed by the intensity of the emotions represented in Caroyl's work, she felt she had to clarify her own role with Caroyl's parents. The parents told the counselor that under no circumstances was it to be confirmed that she was going to die because such a confirmation would destroy Caroyl's will to live. There-

after, Caroyl and the counselor worked together with both knowing, and recognizing the other knew, but not talking openly of her
death.

Although we did not directly discuss her dying, we did talk
about many other things, such as funerals, fear, confidentiality,
faith, truth, and trust. Depending on what and how she asked, the
counselor answered as a helper or friend: the latter when we were
discussing philosophy, more often the former, as when Caroyl was
angry at the lack of privacy in the hospital. The combination of
teaching and counseling one-to-one daily over many months, combined with invitations for the counselor to attend family functions,
changed the boundaries of "pure" school counseling. But no matter what the situation, the counselor is obligated to respond out of
caring and what is best for the child.

Artwork

The main series begins with a drawing, "Spiders," done about
five months after the initial session (fig. 5.1). By this time Caroyl
was established in the self-concept Bluebond-Langner (1978) calls
Stage 3, "always ill but will get better."

The central figure is Caroyl, and this is one of the few drawings
where the story is in the first person, making the ownership of the
symbolic message even more powerful. The mouth is wide open in
what could be taken as a lopsided smile or a scream. The screaming interpretation is more likely, because the story is about being
tricked by people hiding in the bushes, people whom Caroyl
discovers without knowing they were there. In the end, Caroyl
runs home screaming after they put spiders all over her.

The spider represents the Great Weaver or Creator (Cooper,
1978) who spins the thread of life. The figure was initially drawn
without hands, suggesting a sense of powerlessness, and without
the spiders; they were added after the story was dictated. The lines
all over the clothing are later described as "lines from running."
They also make the sweater-dress look as if it is unraveling, suggesting her thread of life is coming undone. Both the right eye and
leg seem somewhat smaller and weaker. The tree is oddly shaped,

FIG. 5.1   Spiders

with a massive trunk and little foliage. This suggests a difficulty getting enough energy to maintain her body. The blue cloud, lined with yellow, may suggest a need to cry, and the beginnings of a rainbow, symbolic bridge between spiritual and temporal, a promise that peace will come. The legs are blue and are in a position called "kicking up his heels" from an earlier drawing, suggesting a fairly strong flow of energy still present.

The overall tone of the story was one of trickery and fear, masked somewhat by a show of brightness. At this time Caroyl was denying the nasty trick of fate ("Why me?") in saying she will "always be ill."

Figure 5.2, "Always Crying," done a week later, is also from Stage 3 and shows her depression. The dramatic elimination of most of the body is accentuated by the shift to using pencil only. Three tears from each eye make the emotional tone obvious. The explanation for the crying included physical hurt, broken promises, not being liked, and not being able to go out. The features on

100

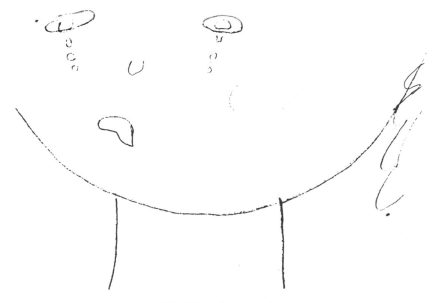

FIG. 5.2   Always crying

the face are placed on the lower half. How would it feel to have the face distorted like that? About an hour before this drawing was done, she told me about her dizziness the night before and how her legs felt like they were not there, immobilizing her. The picture clearly represented the state of the body. Yet, although the girl is "always crying," mirroring "always ill," she erased the neck and drew a larger one. The new one will allow her to hold up her head still, in spite of the painful life she leads right now. Stories and other pictures from this time show movement to the right of the page, in the direction of life, and end with living "happily ever after" or other terms suggesting a happy future.

The large, fierce gorilla in figure 5.3 is in a cage with a mirror and swing. People are throwing fruit and a carrot in for him. Is the carrot the "carrot dangled on a stick"? The picture suggests bargaining, although we cannot be sure of just what the carrot represents. Does the gorilla symbolize caged anger or perhaps the disease? Could the food given to the gorilla represent medicines

FIG. 5.3   Gorilla

taken to hold the disease under control? (Bluebond-Langner indicates that children at this stage are often aware of the medicines
taken as being the same as the ones when first diagnosed and different from those taken later. They also believe that the drugs will
make them well again.) The gorilla, whose face is out of align-
ment, seems to be looking toward the left, turning more toward
the pale yellow mirror. Since both the apple, which is on the left,
and the mirror often symbolize knowledge, one could question
whether Caroyl was moving to a new understanding or awareness
of her condition.

Figure 5.4, "Art Gallery," done two days later, is a trick. A punk
(angry) girl is at the art gallery where she puts graffiti on a picture
which looks like scribbles but is really eyes. On her return visit, an
eye winks and then talks to her. Then she wakes up.

Again the face is badly distorted, perhaps suggesting the difficulty in facing reality. The lack of arms and hands—powerlessness
—combined with the purple suggests a strong need for control or

FIG. 5.4   Art gallery

support from others. The colors chosen for the repeated eyes—
first pale yellow, then orange, yellow-green and finally purple
—emphasize the critical nature of her declining health. The situation is so precarious that a purple frame is needed to contain it.
The trickery of the talking picture in the upper portion of the page
may be the fantasy that the disease is all a trick, yet the reality for
the girl in the lower portion is that she will always be sick. There is
no more happily ever after. The eyes symbolize the faculty of intuitive vision and tell her, "Nobody's tricking you." She is seeing
reality. Now the black, misshapen feet can only plod heavily
along. Bluebond-Langner indicates that, at Stage 4, children see
themselves as "always ill and will never get better." Although attempting to deny it, she now "wakes up" to this new reality.

By the time of the next picture two weeks later, this concept is
firm. The blue door would be hard to get into or out of since it is
so far above the bottom of the house. Her story indicates that the
girl can get in, but must escape through a hole in the roof, imply-

103

ing that only a spiritual escape from her body is possible. She climbs stairs which creak noisily under her weight, giving her away to the ghost who lives here, her earthly part given away to her spirit. The ghost scares her and she wakes up screaming. Again the text includes both a trick and a waking up.

There are three floors, the upper two inhabited by ghosts with no eyes, and six windows, two boarded up and one without glass. This could suggest that on a spiritual or intuitive level she knows what is going on without needing to see it, but her conscious self needs to block out this painful reality. There is no color in the bottom left, supporting the concept of repressed feelings. The black may then symbolize the unknown or the dark future she is not quite ready for. Yet within the black house are dark brown and bright blue, both suggesting health and energy. The three ghosts, who are in windows framed by blue or brown, represent the positive growth potential of her spiritual self. Her faith, always present, became even stronger in these last months.

The next story also includes a dream. The man wakes up and "lives on," but we are not told he gets better or even lives happily. Almost the entire page is a bright blue waterfall, confirming the energy and healthy spirit. This suggests she is still in Stage 4. The flowing water of life here suggests she has reached acceptance of this stage.

Figure 5.5 is included not so much as part of the chronology of the disease, but to emphasize the value of drawing for children. Caroyl's mother had not reached me in time to cancel the morning session. Since the counselor was already there, she asked Caroyl if she would like to do a picture, even though she was too sick for school. She agreed. Her inner self appears even sicker than her face indicates. The location of the figure on the left side of the page and the repetition of tears suggest depression. The title was added verbally at the end, "not feeling well," but written, "not feeling bad." When asked for clarification, she agreed that she did now indeed feel much better, and could we please have school. As we discussed this new idea with her mother, we all became aware of the value of simply drawing pictures.

"The Rabbit Disgoise" [sic] was done six days later. The paper is

earoyl
nat
feeling
bad

FIG. 5.5   Not feeling well

turned vertically this time, making it a stronger statement than the others, and there is a striking similarity to the gorilla done two and a half months earlier. The main characters are in the same place on the page and have a similar stance, although this time the face is clear. But we are told by the title that this is a disguise. Though the carrot is almost identical in placement and shape, the color is lacking. Again, we cannot be sure what the carrot is, although the story says everyone wants this single carrot and the man "loved carrots—you have to remember that." The story also tells us the man eats it after putting on a rabbit suit. The rabbit symbolizes the trickster for American Indians, but putting on a rabbit skin symbolizes docility and humility before the Great Spirit (Storm, 1972). Does this mean, then, that ordinary rabbits moving to the right are not going to get that carrot, but this humble one, turning left, will?

As she drew, Caroyl said, "I used to draw good rabbits, but I don't now. I've changed." She said that she wanted to use only pen, the only drawing in the series done this way. She also told me that her best friend had died two days earlier and said, "She loved me best." The uniqueness of the use of pen and the direction of the paper stress the importance of this drawing. At this point Caroyl has moved into Stage 5, "dying." She has moved through the other views of self and now can connect the death of a friend from the same disease as the logical outcome of her own illness.

"The Flower Bed" was drawn two days later. This is done in pencil, and the paper is returned to the horizontal position. There are three flowers, just as there were three rabbits. One good friend of Caroyl's had died five months before and the other four days before. The crossed-out flower's stem, if extended, would connect with the "l" at the end of her name; she knows at the unconscious level what her own fate is.

The flower on the right was erased and redrawn as a tulip, the symbol for perfect love (Cooper, 1978). The bird groupings are crows, hawks and eagles. The M-shaped birds appearing for the second picture in a row and above the crossed-out flower are the crows. They symbolize the messenger of death from the gods, whereas the other two are both solar and heavenly symbols. Caroyl actually changed her mind about the middle flock, going from robins to hawks. Her two friends were already part of the spiritual world; she was just receiving the message.

Figure 5.6, "The Sad Monster," was done the next day. As a huge three-legged monster approaches from the left asking to be buddies, three tiny humans say yes and one says no. The brown, colored over green, suggests the potential for growth, possibly psychological healing, or coming to terms with death. The purple suggests the power of the monster and perhaps a need for support. Caroyl talked about funerals and remembering as the monster was colored in. As she drew the people, she talked about friendship, describing ours as "hugging good friends." Perhaps the monster represents death. Three parts of her have accepted this, but one part still resists.

Figure 5.7, "The Flat Tire," followed four days later. This time there are four flowers, one sitting secure and three bouncing off the cart when the tire goes flat. Those three, dramatically shaken out of their world, do not reach their vases when the pencil outline

FIG. 5.6　The sad monster

FIG. 5.7　The flat tire

is colored in with felt pen. The stable one does reach the vase. This could refer back to the fact that her body is now three-quarters dead from cancer. The man pulling the cart is on the far side of the handles, so that if he pulled from where he is gripping the one handle only, the cart would reverse its direction and go to the left. This directional change is important in confirming the direction of her life. She has now reversed toward the left and the west or death. Subsequent pictures showing movement are in this direction, whereas all previous ones showed movement to the right, if not facing front. The cart is decorated with three sets of three concentric circles, suggesting perhaps completion of three sets of past, present, and future.

Three months later, she drew a picture of two butterflies, black body representing the chrysalis or death, combined with the emergence of the reborn butterfly. Kubler-Ross (1983) writes of children in concentration camps and many hospitals drawing butterflies. Caroyl put considerable energy into drawing the face on the large one, the pencil outline on the smaller one and the evergreen tree beside it. Both cocoons and the large evergreen are outlined in crayon also. Does the energy used in outlining reflect a concern with her outer world? There are three deciduous trees which are very green, although the season was fall. Does this discrepancy then signify the rebirth of spirit? There are seven flowers, seven being the first number to contain both the spiritual and the temporal (Cooper, 1978, p. 117). The flowers are orange and purple, and the butterfly dots are also these colors, suggesting an intense struggle, the life and death battle her body still fights. All the tree trunks started as a pale yellow, a precarious life situation, and are covered over with black. Does this signify fear of the elimination of each tree's connection with nurturing from the ground, the connection with earth?

Two months later (fig. 5.8) Caroyl draws two evergreens again, one on either side of a "Monster." The monster, done in the pale blue of the sky with purple arms and eyes, at first appears to be frightening to the tiny person who calls for help. Is this death calling for her? The dotted lines of the monster have not appeared before. The lines suggest the breaking down of her own body

FIG. 5.8   Monster

boundaries due to the leukemia. The dark pink navel associates this figure with the Cosmic center and is the connection to the thread of life. The monster is almost framed by green and is above the ground, suspended or rising. If one looks at the house with a sagging door, unaligned roof, a chimney with no smoke or warmth inside, and two intense, uneven windows (the orange of a life–death struggle larger than the green, healthy one), perhaps the person is calling to the monster for help. The monster mouth is blood-red and seems smeared, possibly signifying the need for an infusion of healthy blood.

Because "help" was so obvious, the counselor asked Caroyl if she ever felt like that figure, one of the few times the counselor related picture content beyond the third person. That one opening led to a long discussion about how her family was coping, her wish to talk more, but wanting to protect them from more distress. The lack of windows on the ground floor and the sketchy front of the house could have told us that she had to keep something hidden or could not be "up front." This one question opened our dialogue considerably for this session and future ones.

Figure 5.9, "Robin," was done three days later. Although it was November, Caroyl said she had seen this robin. The bird's body, emerging out of the broken white egg, is the pale blue of the earlier sky, and lines from the wings soar right off the page, perhaps signifying the rising spirit alluded to with the monster. The large pink sections of closed wings suggest being more "in the pink." In Christian symbolism, the robin signifies death and resurrection. The egg, or Cosmic Egg, here shattered and lying around the robin, is yet another symbol of resurrection of the spirit and of hope. The blood-red from the mouth is now on the chest, where it belongs on robin redbreast. Does the golden yellow beak with two nostrils suggest a breathing in of the spiritual? It seems as if acceptance of her lot is beginning.

Figure 5.10 was done one week later. Called "The Land and the Sea," it is accompanied by a story of a princess being carried (to the left) back to the king's castle so she can tell him she is going to marry the slave. The fish, representing the stream of life, are going to the right. The blue of the sky is here the blue of the water also. The brown or healing, earthy color making up over half of the picture was colored over by golden yellow, a spiritual, not earthly, healing. The living creatures, people and fish, are transparent, an image of fading life. This is, then, a pictorial representation of "crossing the waters," as seen in so many cultures both preceding and following death.

Figure 5.11, "Bear and Snowman," done two weeks later, again tells of fading life. The bear took most of the drawing time, with erasing to get the lines faint enough. There was some erasing of the snowman also, to get the head big enough. Of course, the snowman is a very temporary creature who will melt away soon. Both figures have hats on, and the lower floor does not have any windows, suggesting a need to repress or not disclose something. Both figures have the same posture, arms spread open, leaving the body vulnerable. As in so many of Caroyl's pictures, there is a discrepancy with the right eye being smaller. Ears are included here. Much strength went into drawing the sensory organs in the

FIG. 5.9 Robin

FIG. 5.10 The land and the sea

FIG. 5.11   Bear and snowman

snowman. Could the cancer cells have started their interference with sensory receptors in the brain? It is a cloudy, colorless day. Do the cloudiness and the erasing tell us the transition from this world is close? The number six reappears in the number of coals for the mouth, the number of sections in the chimney, and the steps on the walkway. Six weeks to the day, Caroyl was rushed to the hospital for her final admission.

Caroyl then drew a picture called "The Secret Garden." Caroyl was reading the novel of the same name with her mother. The picture suggests chaos or wildness. There is a wall with a door, two firmly rooted trees, the three little flowers from before, and a girl who appears to have just entered the garden. She has two heart-shaped buttons, where the bear had two circles. Does this suggest the physical and spiritual centers are now combined in one, where the dotted monster represented only the spiritual? The two trees touch both sky and ground, symbolizing a joining of heaven and earth in this garden. There are clouds, but they do not block the sun. The left arm dangles strangely from the sleeve, and both arms seem to go straight out from the shoulders to bend at the elbows, a very uncomfortable position to maintain. Does this suggest it is very difficult to maintain the body at all now? The hair and the doorknob are both much darker than all other parts of the picture. Is the hair hiding or holding down something? She penciled in the same hair she usually drew for characters identified with herself, yet filled a much smaller part of it. The knob is visible now, but Caroyl said the ivy (signifying eternal life, being evergreen even in the coldest winter) growing over the wall would make the door nearly impossible to find. The girl would have some difficulty fitting in the door to the garden as she is much bigger than it is. Once in the garden, there's no going back? The wall seems like the barrier between life and death. Caroyl is preparing to die, to go over to the "other side" from which there is no return in this lifetime.

One of the last pictures drawn in the hospital for her parents, "The Setting Sun," shows two separate houses, four birds in the sky, and a car driving toward a setting sun (fig. 5.12). The drawing suggests the final transition from life to death. Her conscious ego and her body, as symbolized by the car, are dying (i.e., heading toward the setting sun). She is leaving her two homes in this world (the home with her family and the home of the hospital) and entering the realm of the spirit as symbolized by the birds flying in the sky. Not only did she achieve peace, she also made certain those who cared clearly saw that peace in symbolic and visual form. Two weeks later, on January 30, 1986, Caroyl died.

Discussion

Although these drawings were done by a terminally ill child, the same process can be used with children in other critical situations. In Caroyl's case, she benefited greatly from the ongoing love of her parents and family, from the counselor's support and from the opportunity to release through drawings and discussions. Surprisingly little overt anger and violence came out in these pictures,

FIG. 5.12   The setting sun

although Bluebond-Langner (1978) and Kiepenheuer (1980) in-dicate these are typical themes of hospitalized, critically ill children. This may be partially a result of the family's provision for effective anger release through a punching doll and a shouting place. Future work to investigate drawings of critically ill children done outside of a hospital setting could be useful.

Some guidelines for the use of art must be followed. All work is to be respected and accepted in a non-judgmental manner. Keeping discussions in the third person helps clarify what is happening but makes recognition of feeling much less threatening. Interpretation may be in the mind of the helper only, but if any connection is made to the drawing content, it should be very open-ended and tentative, giving the child options in responding.

The use of drawings can be valuable to a variety of helpers, from consultants and medical staff in hospitals—especially when somatic aspects are also included—to school counselors and teachers.

Sharing the results offers great comfort to grieving family members and may make a difference in the quality of family communication patterns in the final weeks.

The greater the helper's knowledge of psychology and symbolism, the greater the skill in interpreting content. However, a basic caring and a willingness to be open to the child's view will enable many to be effective in aiding a child on a journey through life.

Chapter 6

EARTH, FIRE, WATER AND SUN: ARCHETYPAL ART EDUCATION WITH SCHOOL CHILDREN

AS COUNSELORS AND art teachers working in the public school system, we are concerned that many children, as they progress through the grade levels, become disillusioned with art and art classes. Many very young children love to draw, paint and doodle, but as they get older the natural pleasure they experience from this process is greatly reduced, and many become critical and fearful of art classes and the art process.

We question the role traditional art education programs, with their emphasis on technique, play in causing these negative experiences. Something is missing for these children who hate art classes and draw little more than stereotyped images. We wonder whether some methods from the field of art therapy might help students overcome their fears, enjoy the art process and produce some original work.

Art Education

Origin

Although drawing became a subject in American schools as early as the 1870s and art appreciation was introduced into school programs by the turn of the century, children's work was not recognized as a genuine form of art until the 1930s. The ideas of the American philosopher and educator John Dewey, in the 1930s, and educator Victor Lowenfeld, in the 1940s and 1950s, laid the foundation for much of the current thinking in the field of art education today.

Dewey believed that the focus of art education should be unlocking the creative energies of children and that children should be active participants in this process. As a result of his work and others', children's art began to be seen as a valid form of art and not just an inferior reflection of the adult world.

Lowenfeld was interested in the psychological aspects of art education. He viewed it as a process, a means to an end, which for him was the development of the individual. His idea that children's art develops in a typical and predictable manner was important in freeing children from the unrealistic expectations of adults. Emphasizing the value of creative art activity for healthy psychological growth, Lowenfield believed that art education and therapy could not be separated and called on art educators to use a therapeutic approach, which he called "art education therapy" (Chapman, 1982; Drachnik, 1976; Lowenfeld in Michael, 1982).

In the last decade, as many art educators have reassessed the goals and practices of art education, they have begun taking another look at the writings of Dewey and Lowenfeld. Their ideas are often used to support efforts to make art education a more vital and creative field of study.

Purpose

Art education's primary aim, according to Lowenfeld, should be to develop a child's sensitivity toward the self and the world, in this way helping him or her to become a useful member of society. One of the most important tasks of art education is to cultivate a child's natural creative potential (Lowenfeld in Michael, 1982).

The purpose of art education for Seonaid Robertson (1982) is not to make the students artists, but rather to give them the experience of being absorbed in an activity which will take them down through the layers of their own personalities and extend their levels of experience.

In the view of the art educator Gottfried Tritten (1964), art

117

education must help children to gain experience, order that experience, and express it in clear, distinct images. Children's art, he thinks, is a manifestation of their attempts to assimilate their experiences and master their reality.

Laura Chapman, another well-known art educator, thinks that a good education in art would prepare children for "enlightened citizenship in a democratic society" (Chapman, 1982, p. 38). It would enable young people to understand art as part of their cultural heritage and to make informed decisions about its role in their lives. It would give children the opportunity to develop general skills and attitudes which would be useful throughout their lives, whether or not they chose careers in art.

Current Issues

Several issues have been debated by art educators for many years—the role of the art teacher, the importance of teaching technique, and the significance of the subject matter.

Role of the Teacher. It is the teacher's responsibility to create a nonjudgmental atmosphere in which children can relax their defenses, express themselves freely, and yet at the same time treat others with respect (Pine, 1975). Chapman (1982) urges art teachers to see their role as one of extending their students' knowledge of the arts beyond their ability to create art. As tasks of the teacher, she includes planning a program consisting of a wide variety of in-class lessons, several field trip possibilities, and opportunities for displaying and discussing finished work.

An important job of the teacher, according to Robertson (1982), is to help each individual develop his or her own language of expression in art. This process requires considerable sensitivity on the part of the teacher. The teacher must know when it is appropriate to teach students new skills, draw their attention to works of art by the masters or let them create on their own.

There are times when some children have difficulty expressing themselves and resort to constricted, repetitive stereotyped images. The way the teacher chooses to deal with this issue could permanently affect a child's attitude to art. Many art educators have addressed this important problem.

In defense of stereotyped images, Kramer (1975), both an art teacher and psychotherapist, notes they may help the child ward off the emotional upheaval that may follow creative work and thereby help maintain the individual's equilibrium. The teacher's role is not so much to free the child from these inhibitions, but to "help chaotic fantasy develop into imagination and to revive an atrophied faculty of observation and self observation" (p. 40).

Lowenfeld also warns against diverting the child away from the stereotype, for this could cause the child to feel insecure and frustrated (in Michael, 1982). Instead, he encourages teachers to try to make the stereotype alive and meaningful to the child. Teachers could make the experience the child is trying to portray more vivid by asking questions about details of the experience or, if possible, by helping the child to act it out in the safety of the classroom. Robertson (1982) suggests that a child could be given a different material to work with or helped to look carefully at new aspects of the subject.

Churchill (1971) has several ideas for overcoming blocks to creative expression. The teacher should encourage, as a general rule, experimentation and individual differences in style and should provide many firsthand experiences. Direct observation from real life or teaching a particular technique can often help free a child from stereotypes. If a child is constantly copying, the teacher could ask the child to use the copied images in an imaginative context.

Role of Technique. A lot of controversy in the field of art education concerns the extent to which techniques should be taught to children. At one end of the art education spectrum are programs which focus exclusively on a disciplined study of techniques, and at the other end are programs which, in addition to teaching technique, include many opportunities for creative, imaginative expression.

Chapman (1982) is extremely critical of those who believe that teaching art to young children is unnecessary and potentially damaging. In her view, very young children have natural artistic ability, but around the fourth grade when their self-confidence in making art declines, skill development is very important. Learning skills helps children feel more competent, and this, she feels, increases their self-confidence.

While Chapman is critical of programs which underestimate the value of technique, Robertson (1982) is wary of those which give it too much emphasis. She believes techniques should be taught not for their own sake, but to facilitate the creative process. Knowing how to paint but not having anything to say in the painting, in Robertson's opinion, contributes nothing to the common good. Robertson looks for a balance between technique and what technique is developed to say. She suggests that within the art program there needs to be an alternation between free expression of spontaneous feeling and exercises in which different media are explored or certain techniques are perfected.

For Tritten (1964), techniques are a means to an end. If learning techniques helps to stimulate children's creativity and expressiveness and helps build their confidence, then it is a worthwhile exercise. In cases where children do not have the technical ability to express themselves, learning techniques can be of great assistance, according to Champernowne (1971). Technical competence can be a support and can help the child give form to the inner creative process.

Role of Subject Matter. Differences of opinion about subject matter seem to center around the importance attributed to the process of tapping the child's inner world through art. Most art educators encourage children to look to the external world for a source of images for their art. Tritten (1964) is one of the few who believe that there can be no real success in art unless the subject is the key to a child's interior world and can fire his or her imagination.

Subject matter is so important to Robertson (1982) that she made it the focus of extensive research. Her hypothesis was that relevant topics inspired children to produce evocative or haunting artwork. Robertson found that there were some themes which produce in the artist an intense state of concentration and a deep sense of satisfaction with the product. These archetypal themes had a timeless quality and could offer "a vertical path back into the core of oneself" (p. 89).

The subject must interest the children and be able to carry them through to a new synthesis. In creating art, ". . . we are brought face to face with the mystery of the self which is shaped in the act of shaping material things and created anew in the act of creating" (Robertson, 1982, p. 107).

Criticism of Current Practices

Current practices in art education are extremely diverse, and some have been severely criticized. Some of the alternative programs that have grown out of these criticisms embody a wide range of different approaches.

Kramer (1975) wrote about what she called "the perversion of modern art education." In her view, the desire for easy prescriptions and fear of the unpredictable have led many art educators away from efforts to stimulate creative work and toward what she calls "pseudo art activities" (p. 37). Instead of extensive exploration of each medium, children are exposed briefly and superficially to many different techniques. Novelty, rather than depth of experience and knowledge, in her opinion, too often becomes the goal.

Laura Chapman (1982), another outspoken critic of art education in American public schools, blames art teachers for offering students "instant art"—activities which require little skill, knowledge, effort and time, and thereby encourage children to regard art as frivolous. Chapman is critical of many educators who narrowly define art education as simply the making of art. For Chapman, creating art is only one aspect of art education. Children must learn how to respond to art as well. She is also opposed to the common practice of integrating art with other subjects, believing that this dilutes its study.

Alternatives

The programs of Laura Chapman and Seonaid Robertson stand in sharp contrast to the approaches criticized above. While not the only such alternatives, they do provide ways to make art education more meaningful.

Chapman (1982) believes that art is a subject requiring study, and she has developed a comprehensive curriculum, the *Discover Art* series for elementary school children. Her ideas are currently being introduced to some North American schools and represent an important trend in art education.

In Chapman's program, children study art from the point of view of both the creator and the perceiver. They consider the social and historical dimensions of art as they become aware of their artistic heritage and the role of art in society. The lessons draw on and expand the knowledge and experience of the children as they develop the skills with which to express themselves. One year of the program offers children a wide variety of art experiences. In the process of learning skills involved in painting, drawing, making sculpture and using color, children are exposed to different forms and styles of art, from the time of the cave dwellers to the present.

Robertson (1982) shares with Chapman the understanding that teaching the visual arts must occur within a wider sphere of knowledge and experience—a sphere that includes the past, the present and the future. But Robertson's approach differs from Chapman's in its emphasis. Robertson views art education in the context of a world in turmoil, in which the development of the human soul has not been a priority. She believes that art should be a vehicle for finding a way to one's center, and art teachers should facilitate that process. In her art lessons, the process is the key rather than the final product, as she helps children reach down into their cores to find meaningful self-expression.

Robertson chooses subjects that draw on the life experiences and aspirations of the children she teaches. Because she believes that the basis of all art is in sensation, Robertson designs physical activities involving the children so that they may more fully experience what they are trying to express. For example, one project she did with fifteen-year-old working class boys in a coal mining town in England included making a mine in the classroom. The topic was chosen as a result of a discussion in which the boys indicated that they would probably all be miners when they left school. Before they began painting and sculpting the theme, they tried to simulate the experience of being in a mine by crawling through a dark and narrow makeshift tunnel in the classroom. This provided them with a wider range of experience and feeling to draw on when they expressed themselves through their art.

Both Chapman and Robertson are interested in broadening the scope of art education and in encouraging children to experience art in the context of the world around them. But Robertson takes this one step further in her efforts to help children tap the wealth of resources within themselves, enriching their artwork in the process. It is Robertson's ideas that stimulated this present study.

Method

In this project, elementary school children were asked to respond in art form to four archetypal themes—Earth, Fire, Water and Sun. Preparatory discussion and guided imagery were used to stimulate their involvement in the art process. The children interpreted the themes by expressing images on paper, which were later viewed and discussed by the class.

Objectives of the Project. The goal of this project was to deepen the art experience for both student and teacher, stimulating and involving children in the art process by giving them an opportunity to express a personal response to basic elements in their own lives as well as those of people throughout history. To encourage the children to develop their own imagery instead of relying on stereotyped or copied art products, a safe, non-threatening environment was created in which every sincere response was acceptable. Other important objectives of this project were to emphasize free expression, rather than the development of skills, and to provide the teacher with an opportunity to gain more insight into the emotional and psychological well-being of the students.

Population and Sampling Procedures. A total of ninety-five children from grades four to seven were involved in this study. They were enrolled in three different elementary schools, referred to here as School A, School B and School C. These schools were chosen because they are located in different parts of the city of Vancouver, Canada, and in different types of communities. It was felt that this factor might provide some interesting comparisons when results were analyzed. School A consisted of many children from single-parent families, School B contained mostly children from two-parent families, and School C had children with behavior problems in the intermediate special classes (ages nine to twelve years).

The time spent with each class varied. One class worked on all four themes, while the others were presented with only one or two themes. It was important that each theme be allotted one uninterrupted time block. Eighty minutes (one double art period) was usually enough time to complete all stages of the activity. These sessions took place over a two-year period. Grade 6/7 and the special remedial classes were involved one year, and the two other classes participated the following year. If the class worked on more than one theme, sessions were scheduled at one-week intervals.

Selection of Topics. Selecting appropriate themes was crucial to the success of the project. The themes had to be relevant to children of all cultural backgrounds and to be capable of evoking strong associations and images. Seonaid Robertson believes that there are some universal themes, archetypal themes, which can activate intense associations, inspire the artist to create evocative artwork and profoundly affect the human psyche. Influenced by these ideas we chose four themes—Earth, Fire, Water, and Sun—which have been essential elements in the lives of all people of all times. Since everyone has had some experience with each of these elements, it was thought that this would facilitate the image-making process.

Materials. Very basic art supplies are the only materials necessary for this project. Paper and crayons or pastels are sufficient, but paint and brushes offer more choice and an opportunity for freer and bolder expression. All the materials, except for the brushes, were handed out before the project officially began, to avoid interrupting the flow of images. The brushes are too much of a temptation for children who tend to fiddle nervously with things, and so they were handed out when it was time to begin working.

Implementation

First Stage: Stimulation through Discussion

The project began with a whole class discussion aimed at stimulating and focusing the children's imaginations. The children were asked what creativity is, what it means to use one's imagination, and what a creative, imaginative work of art would look like. The purpose of this discussion was to encourage the students to use their own imaginations and to focus on their own responses, rather than what they perceived to be the expectations of their peers or teacher. When the same class later worked on other themes, a quick reminder to use their imaginations was sufficient at the outset of the session.

Following this, the name of the theme—Earth, Fire, Water or Sun—was written on the board. The children were then asked to share with the class whatever associations came immediately to mind. This was an important part of the discussion, and the teacher's task was to elicit as many associations and images as possible.

Second Stage: Relaxation and Guided Imagery

At the end of the discussion, the teacher summarized the range of views. Then the children were asked to close their eyes, rest

125

their heads and listen to the words spoken as the teacher walked around the room inducing relaxation and activating images of the particular theme selected. These words were said slowly, in a very calm, relaxed voice.

If some children still had their eyes open, the teacher remarked that it can be scary to close one's eyes and that sometimes it takes a few moments to feel comfortable enough to do it. The teacher further stated that no one would be pressured to close his or her eyes, but doing so makes it easier to shut out all the distractions, focus on what is inside, and allow images to form in the mind. Once most of the children relaxed, the teacher introduced the guided imagery for each theme (see below). When this was finished, the teacher moved to the next phase.

Third Stage: Artwork

When the children were ready and an image had formed in their minds, they opened their eyes and expressed those images on the paper in front of them. They were encouraged not to discuss what they were doing with their classmates and not to look at each other's work until this part of the activity was finished. This helped the less motivated or less confident students to avoid being too influenced by the ideas of their classmates and to express images of their own. Throughout this stage, the teacher walked around the room encouraging all students in their efforts.

If any child had difficulty getting started, he or she was asked to shut his or her eyes again and think over what had been said in the guided imagery until an image came into focus. If a child asked, "Is this good?" he in turn was asked, "Does it make *you* feel good? Are you pleased with it?" If he or she was, nothing further was said. If the child was not satisfied, the teacher asked what he or she needed to do in the painting in order to feel better about it. Every effort was made to direct the focus back to the student, to encourage the child to trust herself rather than look to the teacher for approval.

Fourth Stage: Viewing and Discussing the Products

When the artwork was finished, the children had an opportunity to look at their classmates' work. They either left their work on their desks and walked around the room looking at the other drawings and paintings, or, one at a time, each child held up his or her work for the whole class to see. In both cases, a discussion followed in which the children were encouraged to share their responses to the artworks. During these discussions, the teacher underscored those comments that took note of the wide range of possible interpretations of the same theme and reinforced the efforts of those individuals who chose to interpret the theme in unusual ways. This encouraged the children to trust their own ideas and not to be afraid of expressing themselves differently than their friends.

Evaluation

The project was evaluated in two steps. First, the students' response at each stage of the project and to each theme was assessed. Then these results were compared by theme and by class.

Method of Analysis. There is a subjective and an objective component of the analysis. When the children's artwork was examined and categorized by its content and assessed for its artistic merit, a subjective judgment was being made. This judgment was based upon years of experience as an art teacher and training as a counselor. Once numbers were assigned to the various categories, the process became more objective (see below).

Student Response at Each Stage of Implementation. Student reactions at each of the four stages of implementation were assessed in order to determine the degree to which the children were involved in the activity. Some of the factors considered included the interest and enthusiasm shown by the children in the initial discussion, their willingness to relax and follow the guided imagery, the focus of their energy during the artwork stage (on their own art or their friends'), and their interest in discussing the art of their classmates.

127

Student Response to Themes. In evaluating this project, it was important to know if the themes captured the interest of the children, if the themes triggered an emotional response, either positive or negative, and if some archetypal themes stirred up more feelings than others. To help answer these questions, it was necessary to categorize the images produced. Four categories were selected to describe the ways in which the themes were interpreted—"positive," "negative," "ambivalent," and "neutral."

The positive category included images which emphasized the life-giving, healing, nurturing or enjoyable aspects of the element. The negative category consisted of those images which portrayed the element's destructive, damaging or painful characteristics. Images with both positive and negative features were classified as ambivalent, and those with no apparent affect were placed in the neutral category.

Each work of art was examined and placed in the most appropriate category, based on the subject of the painting, its style and the feelings it evoked, and the student's own comments about his or her work.

The artistic merit of each drawing or painting was also assessed. The artwork was considered "successful" if it was creative and well-executed or exceptionally imaginative. The images were placed in two categories—"original" or "stereotyped or copied." The latter category included images which were mechanical representations, often overly reliant on earlier developmental forms and lacking a sense of individual expression, or were images copied from other children.

Once the images were categorized, numbers for each category were totaled and turned into percentages which could then be used to compare the results. To determine the most common images for each theme, the subjects chosen by each class were listed and assigned one point every time that image reappeared. From this list, the subjects most often chosen were readily visible.

Results

First Stage: Opening Discussion

In each class there were children who understood what using one's imagination and creativity entailed. Their explanations helped define the concepts for the others. They also helped to clarify our expectations for the class, particularly that the students would focus on developing their own images. In all the classes, students were eager to talk about their associations to the archetypal themes, and always many unique ideas were expressed.

Second Stage: Relaxation and Guided Imagery

Most students got noticeably more relaxed from session to session and followed more closely what was being said. Some had trouble keeping their eyes closed. In each class there were at least one or two children, more in the older class, who had this difficulty. The older children were more comfortable with this process when they worked on their second theme.

Third Stage: Artwork

By the time they were asked to open their eyes, after the relaxation and imagery, most children had images in their minds and were eager to transfer them to paper. But there were one or two hesitant children at this stage in each class, and several in the upper grades (6/7), who "couldn't think of anything." They were asked to relax, close their eyes, think over the images that came up during the guided imagery and choose the one they saw most clearly. For every one of those students, this repetition of the instructions on a one-to-one basis was all that was necessary and they quickly went to work.

The older children seemed to need more reassurance than the younger ones that what they were doing was "acceptable." Some of the grade 6/7 children were concerned that the images they started out with had turned into something else when they had finished. We discussed how this often happens in creative activities when we relax and express what is inside of us and that sometimes we just have to let this process happen, not be frustrated by it, and try to accept the final product in its new form.

Occasionally, in art class, children sitting beside each other will paint or draw very similar pictures. Incidents of copying or being influenced by their neighbors occurred in every class but involved only one or two students each.

When we compared the responses of each class sampled, the overall reaction of the students was positive and enthusiastic. Once the artwork began, the children became very engrossed and worked quietly.

The younger children (grade 4/5 and fifth-grade classes) tended to immerse themselves in the task more readily than the older ones, who took a little longer to settle down, especially with their first experience. When they did settle down, they seemed to enjoy the activity.

The younger children were less inhibited and more spontaneous in their expression than were the older ones, and the students from School B (the ones with the most stable home environment) approached this project with a greater degree of confidence than the others. These students were the most enthusiastic, working very quickly and finishing their artwork in much less time than the other classes.

Fourth Stage: Viewing and Discussing the Products

This was a very valuable part of the process. Whether the students walked around the room to view each other's work or, one at a time, showed and explained their work to the whole class, all the children displayed great interest in their classmates' art and seemed to appreciate the wide range of interpretations. The realization that all interpretations were acceptable had a liberating effect, especially for those children who had felt very insecure about their products. These students were then able to work more confidently on their subsequent themes.

Specific Themes and Guided Imagery

Earth

INTRODUCTORY DISCUSSION

Today we're going to think about earth. What comes into your mind when you think of earth? . . . Look for the two meanings of earth—the world and dirt, soil. Now I'd like you to close your eyes. I will continue talking to you, going over imagery about earth and pausing every now and again so that your imaginations can roam.

RELAXATION AND IMAGERY

Put your head down on your arms or desk and become aware of how you are feeling in your body. Move around a little until you become comfortable. Now become aware of your breathing . . . breathe in and then breathe out. See if you can slow your breathing down a little . . . breathe in slowly and out slowly. Become aware of feeling very relaxed. . . . Now that you are relaxed you can listen to my voice.

You've all had experiences with earth. As I take you on an imaginary journey, some of the experiences may be familiar. You may have been to different parts of the earth or seen them on TV or in movies. Imagine you're in the desert. Look around you. See the very dry sand. Listen to the sounds. How does your skin feel? Now imagine you're deep in the jungle. Everything is very moist and green. And now you're in the cold Arctic. All around you is ice and snow. We're traveling now to the highest parts of the earth high up in the mountains. What can you see? And now we're going down deep into the earth—to the earth's center. How do you feel?. . . What does it look like? We journey to the earth's surface to get a closer look at the soil or dirt. Can you see anything moving in the soil? What does the soil smell like? Feel like? Is anything growing in it? Perhaps you've planted a garden. I bet all of you have experienced getting stuck in the mud, or maybe you've even rolled in the mud. Maybe you've felt the earth's surface shake or seen it crack in an earthquake.

Think about what you like most about the earth, dislike most about the earth. Maybe you've had fantasies about the earth. Let all these images fly through your mind, and let whichever one *stands out* for you come into focus. When you're ready, open your eyes and let this picture come into your paper.

Response to the Theme

This theme elicited both strong positive (fifty-four percent), negative (twenty-one percent) and ambivalent images (nineteen percent). Common images were volcanoes and the earth blowing up. Interestingly, the younger children (nine and ten year olds) drew some form of an aerial view of the earth or a view of the earth from space. From an artistic perspective, most of the pictures were judged both successful and original. Two paintings were stereotyped, and three children copied each other. The younger children had considerably stronger positive associations to Earth than the older children who gave many ambivalent responses.

Fire

INTRODUCTORY DISCUSSION

We're going to let our imaginations think about fire. What comes into your mind when you think of fire? What is fire? Where does it come from?

RELAXATION AND IMAGERY

Just to get our imaginations working smoothly, I want you to sit comfortably, close your eyes, and breathe in slowly . . . in and out . . . in . . . and out. . . .

Now I want you to let your time clock turn backward to take you back in time. I wonder if you can imagine you are one of the first human beings on earth. You have just seen fire for the first time. What does it look like? How does it make you feel? What are the people around you doing and feeling? How will you use the fire? Will you use it for light? For heat? For cooking? For protection from animals? Look around you in the distance. Are there any volcanoes? Do you see a fire-like substance spilling out? What kind of stories will you tell about the magic of fire?

Let pictures form in your mind, almost like you're watching a movie screen. Now let your time clock move ahead slowly to today. Let pictures float across the screen and think about fire today. . . . Maybe you've been camping and have built a campfire. Just smell those hotdogs and marshmallows roasting over the fire. Listen to the sounds the fire makes. I bet you've huddled around a campfire when you were really cold. Imagine you're there now. How does it make you feel? How does the fire look? I wonder if you've ever been stuck in the dark somewhere and someone's used fire to light your way—maybe a torch or match to help you see. Maybe you've seen the big fires at the beach when all the Christmas trees are burned. Can you see it on your screen? What does it look like? Sound like?. . . Smell like?

Think what you like about fire, how it helps you. . . . Let the pictures come into your mind as you breathe slowly in . . . and slowly out.

Now let's think about fire in a different way. Have you ever seen fire get out of control? What did that fire look like? What did it do? How did you feel? Maybe you've been hurt by a fire or seen other people hurt by a fire. Let pictures come on your screen. Think about what you don't like about fire . . . breathing in and out . . . in and out. . . .

I wonder if you've ever dreamed about fire or had any fantasies about fire. Think for a minute and see if any pictures come on your screen.

I bet lots of different pictures of fire come across your screen today. *Which picture* sticks in your mind more than the others? Let that picture come into focus. In a few moments I'm going to ask you to open your eyes and draw that picture on the paper in front of you.

Remember what it means to use your imagination. Let your

image or picture come on the paper. When you're ready, you can open your eyes and begin your fire pictures.

Response to the Theme

The guided imagery and art activities were all enthusiastically received. The most popular images were volcanoes, forest fires, discovering the first fire, campfires, fireplaces, and houses on fire. Of the total sample, forty-nine percent of the children had negative or destructive interpretations of fire, while forty-one percent emphasized the positive aspects. Ten percent of the images contained both positive and negative components.

All of the students in the remedial class drew scenes of violence, destruction and loss of control. Artistically, very few stereotyped images were produced, and many paintings showed creativity and originality.

Water

INTRODUCTORY DISCUSSION

Today we're going to let our imaginations play with water. When you think of water, what's the first thing that comes into your mind?

RELAXATION AND IMAGERY

To get our imaginations working smoothly, I want you to sit comfortably, close your eyes, and breathe in slowly. . . . Let the breath out slowly . . . in and out . . . in . . . and out . . . in . . . and out. . . . Now I'd like you to think about water. As I talk, let pictures come into your mind like you're watching a movie screen. Think of all the different kinds of water, as you are breathing in . . . and out. . . .

Imagine the feeling of rain falling on your skin or being caught in a downpour, getting soaked . . . or think about the fresh, rushing water of a river. What does it sound like? How does the water taste?. . . Maybe you've been swimming in the ocean. Can you imagine yourself there? What does the water taste like?. . . Can you see anything in the water? I wonder if you can actually feel in your body what it's like to float on top of the water . . . or go down into the water and let your skin feel what it's like to be totally covered in water.

Think of all the different sounds water can make as you breathe slowly in and out . . . in and out.

And now let your mind think about all the fun you can have with water. Just let pictures float across your screen. . . . Maybe you're playing games in the water. Maybe you're on a water slide or running through a sprinkler in the summer. Let images come into your mind.

Sometimes water isn't so much fun. Think about what it feels like to be without water—to be so, so thirsty and no water to drink. Or maybe you can remember a time when you had too much water. . . . Have you ever swallowed too much water in a pool or in the ocean? How did that feel? . . . Have you ever almost drowned? I wonder if you've ever been caught in a huge downpour of rain or a tropical monsoon. Or maybe you've experienced a flood or seen one on TV. Can you imagine how you'd feel about water then?

I wonder if you've ever dreamed about water or fantasized about it. Think for a minute and see if any images or pictures come on your screen. Maybe you know some stories about water, like Noah's Ark or Robinson Crusoe or lots of others.

Just let pictures move across your screen. There may be *one picture* that you see more clearly than others. Let that image come into focus . . . and when you're ready, open your eyes and let it come on the paper in front of you.

Response to the Theme

On the whole, this theme elicited mostly positive images (seventy-one percent), while only eighteen percent responded with negative ones. Waterfalls, mountain lakes and streams, swimming and sunsets were common. The negative images involved were drowning and pollution. This activity was useful for inducing calm, restful feelings in many children, especially the younger ones. It also resulted in several artistically successful and original pictures.

135

Sun

INTRODUCTORY DISCUSSION

Let's think about the sun. What's the first thing that comes into your mind? . . . What do you know about the sun?

RELAXATION AND IMAGERY

Now close your eyes. . . . Let pictures form in your mind as I talk. What do you think early human beings thought about the sun? Imagine you are one of those people. What is that mysterious ball of light that moves across the sky, changes color and shape, and then suddenly disappears? What does it look like when you wake up? How different does it look in the middle of the day and at the end of the day? When the sun disappears, everything is so cold and dark. So powerful is the sun. Think of stories you could tell about that strange, warm light. . . .

Now imagine it is 1986 [this year]. . . . How important is the sun in your life. Think of all the ways the sun helps us. Have you ever seen plants lean over trying to get more of the sun's light? Maybe you've helped your father hang clothes outside to dry in the sun. Or maybe you've lain on a towel to dry off in the hot sun at the beach, the lake, or an outdoor pool. . . . Imagine how you feel when the warm sun is on your back. What does it feel like? . . . Maybe you've seen how the sun heats water in tanks on roofs of houses in some countries.

But sometimes the sun can cause harm. Think about a time when your skin got burned from being in the sun too long. Can you remember how that felt? . . . Have you ever seen plants that died from too much sun? . . . Or people wandering, lost in the desert as the sun beats down and there's no water or shade in sight?

Have you ever dreamed about the sun or had some wild fantasies about it? Think for a minute and see if any pictures come into your mind. . . . As you consider what you really like and don't like about the sun, there may be *one image* that you see more clearly than the others. Let that image come into focus.

When you're ready, open your eyes and put that picture on the paper in front of you.

Response to the Theme

The majority of the students (sixty-two percent) had positive images of and associations to the sun. Most common were a large picture of the sun itself, the sun's heat and a view of the sun in space. All the children drew or painted original images, and sixty percent of the products were judged to be artistically successful.

Discussion

The Earth theme stimulated a broader range of associations than the other themes. There were forty-one different Earth images, thirty-eight Sun images, thirty-seven Water images and twenty-six Fire images. With respect to the types of images produced, the majority of the children had positive responses to Water, Earth and Sun. But by far the greatest number of positive interpretations was generated by the Water theme (thirteen percent more than the number generated by the Sun theme, which had the next most positive response).

Stimulating the most negative responses, Fire was the only theme with a majority of such responses. Ambivalent responses were expressed most often to the Earth theme (nineteen percent) and then to Fire (twelve percent). There was less ambivalence in the children's interpretations of the Water and Sun themes (nine percent). The Sun theme generated the greatest number of neutral responses (fourteen percent). Fire had the least (none!).

If an ambivalent response reflects conflicting feelings toward a theme and a neutral response shows little feeling at all, one might hypothesize that the themes with the fewest ambivalent or neutral associations are those to which the children had the strongest, most definite reactions. If we assume this to be the case, then the children had the clearest, most conflict-free responses to Fire and Water.

137

Comparison by Class

The grade 6/7 class had different responses to each theme. They had a mixed response to Earth—an even split between positive and negative, and quite a number of ambivalent reactions. But they had a very positive, less ambivalent response to Water.

The grade 4/5 class at the same school had a much more positive response to both Water and Earth than did the 6/7 class. Most of the class had positive associations with Sun, but the majority had a negative response to Fire.

The grade 4/5 and 6/7 classes were very similar in character. Both classes had many active, attention-seeking, articulate children, and both were a challenge to control. But there were differences in their responses to the themes.

The fifth-grade class at School B was better behaved and situated in a more stable community. Though the children responded positively to both Fire and Sun, their reaction to Sun was considerably stronger than to Fire. In this group, associations with both themes were more positive than those of their counterparts in the grade 4/5 class at School A, but even their positive reaction was toned down in response to Fire.

The special remedial class only worked on the Fire theme. As was mentioned earlier in this study, their predominantly negative response seemed to reflect their negative feelings about their lives.

When we look for factors to explain these results, we find that the archetypal themes themselves had an effect that outweighed the influence of the particular class's character. For example, the positive responses to Water came from two somewhat negative (in terms of behavior and attitude) classes. Fire tended to bring out fiery, out-of-control images even in the most positively affected class. It seemed to provide the children with an acceptable way to express their fiery feelings. The images expressed in response to Fire by the grade 4/5 class did appear to mirror their "explosive" behavior in class, and yet their responses to the other themes were positive.

The project encouraged the children to develop their own imagery instead of relying on stereotyped products: almost all of them created original artworks. The children did understand that the emphasis was on free expression, not technique, and they were able to work boldly, without excessive preoccupation to create the perfect picture.

It is difficult to assess objectively whether the project provided the students with a deeper art experience. Judging from their artwork and the images that emerged, the students were very involved in the activity. It had some meaning for them, and they seemed to derive a sense of satisfaction from the process.

For the researchers, it was a meaningful art experience that generated richer images than many other art activities in which the children had been engaged. The artworks provided the researchers with a deeper understanding of the children and some insights into their psychological and emotional well-being.

Evaluation from an Art Therapy Perspective

Here we must consider the therapeutic and diagnostic value of the project, its success at stimulating uninhibited expression in a supportive environment, and its emphasis on the process rather than the final product. From this perspective, the project enhanced the therapeutic experience of using art materials to express oneself freely.

The themes themselves can also have a therapeutic effect. The project results show that the Fire theme apparently served as a vehicle for expressing fiery feelings. It could be used as a means to tap the inner turmoil and anger of the children. If these feelings persisted, perhaps in the form of angry outbursts, the Fire theme could be worked with for a period of time. A second (or third) Fire session could be added in which the children might choose a particularly fiery part of their first painting, enlarge it, and/or paint it in greater detail in a second painting. Or they might be given the opportunity to create fiery paintings until they no longer felt so inclined. When the fiery feelings have subsided, they are ready to move on. At this point, the Water theme, with its soothing, calming effect on the psyche, could be beneficial. Or perhaps it could be used at an earlier stage to calm fiery feelings.

This project clearly has therapeutic benefits, and it is a gold mine for someone interested in diagnosis. Since the images and style with which the children choose to express themselves are often metaphors for their current emotional and psychological states, the pictures from this project are very useful tools in deepening one's understanding of these particular children.

For example, one Fire picture epitomizes the conflict the artist had been experiencing for many months. The boy had had a very difficult time controlling his temper, frequently ending up in fights on the school grounds. His picture shows an animal-like monster jumping out of a fire. The monster is so powerful it breaks through a building. Someone runs out of a house, tries to defeat the monster with water and finally succeeds. This boy had been struggling hard to control and defeat his own "monster," and by the end of the year he had made considerable progress.

Another child with a similar difficulty in controlling angry outbursts chose to interpret the Fire theme by dividing the page in half. One part, representing the past, depicts a man calling for help as lava, fire and hot rocks spew from the volcano beside him. The other part, representing the present, shows the man smiling as he stands beside a neatly built fire, happy now that he can control it.

The artist was a tough fourth-grade girl who was often mistaken for a boy. She had been counseled once a week for ten months two years prior, and the following year one of us was her classroom teacher. Our focus in counseling had been to "soften her up" and to help her deal with her anger in a more constructive manner. When she drew this picture, she was definitely moving in this direction, though it was months before other teachers noticed the change. The images in her artwork not only reflected her current turmoil but also seemed to represent metaphorically changes and growth that had yet to occur on a conscious level outside of counseling.

From an art therapy viewpoint, the project was successful. The artworks were full of material from which to derive valuable insights for diagnostic purposes, though only a few of many examples have been mentioned. The only negative factor that became evident was the time restraint that affects any artwork in a school setting. It is very difficult to encourage free expression and at the same time insist that it occur within a restricted time framework. This problem had less to do with the project itself than with the school setting. Although the project works well enough in this setting, optimum conditions would allow for flexible time periods.

Evaluation from an Art Education Perspective

In this case, it is important to consider both the creative process and the art product. Our results provide evidence of the value of the Earth, Fire, Water, Sun project for stimulating creativity and producing effective artwork. After looking at the pictures created for each theme, no one can doubt that the children's imaginations were actively engaged. The students were encouraged to respond to the four elements in their own unique styles, and these efforts were reinforced throughout the process. Risk-taking and experimenting with new ideas and methods were emphasized as important steps in the process of artistic growth.

The artwork reflected the project's focus on the creative process and free expression. There were many different interpretations of the themes and very little reliance on stereotyped images. Although the purpose of the project was not to emphasize technique, most of the art products were well-executed.

Many beautiful pictures were produced, and some were particularly imaginative. For example, a fifth-grade girl responded to Fire with an image of a large eyeball with a fire reflected in its center; a boy drew an exploding volcano (fig. 6.1). A fifth-grade boy chose to paint sparks and smoke coming out of two toy robots fighting in a toy store, under a Chinese sign (fig. 6.2). Water inspired a seventh-grade girl to draw a very creative picture of mountains reflected in a sink (fig. 6.3) and a boy to depict drowning (fig. 6.4). Responding to Earth, a seventh-grade boy created a nuclear holocaust, full of horror and rage—burning cities, pain, war and a scared man who wants it all to stop but feels helpless. The picture was an expression of his feelings of fear and helplessness about what the world is coming to (fig. 6.5). The Sun made a fifth-grade boy think of a car race on a sunny day, the sun drying the mud into sand (fig. 6.6). These are only a few examples from a very wide range of images stimulated by the four themes.

The project succeeded in providing the children with an excellent outlet for their creativity, but could also be used as a vehicle for learning about technique. One way to explore technique would be to introduce it during the *Viewing and Discussing* stage of the project. As the children consider their classmates' pictures, they could choose which images are impressive and then try to determine what makes them effective. This could lead to a discussion of all or some of the many elements involved in a successful composition. For example, a lesson might focus on how space or color was used in the paintings, or on the ways of creating movement or different moods in a picture. Following this discussion, students could then practice some of these techniques and methods.

The purpose of encouraging the children to analyze each other's art from a technical point of view would be to help them improve their skills. It is extremely important that these discussions not just single out a few "good" examples, for this could discourage the other children from developing their own unique styles and could inhibit their expressiveness. This focus on technique should not occur during the other stages of the activity, because this, too, would be inhibiting. In order for this project to succeed, there has to be an opportunity for the children to respond to the themes and create their artwork in an unself-conscious way.

An important advantage of this project in a school context is that it can be used with a whole class. However, as is the case with many school activities, a smaller group of children would allow for more individual attention and more time for each child to speak in the discussions.

FIG. 6.1   Exploding volcano

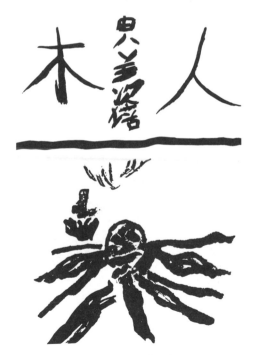

FIG. 6.2   Sparks

FIG. 6.3   Mountain reflection

FIG. 6.4   Drowning

FIG. 6.5   Nuclear holocaust

FIG. 6.6   Car race

Chapter 7

COMMON SYMBOLS OF CHILDREN IN ART COUNSELING

BEFORE WE SUGGEST some possible interpretations of the more common symbols used by children, a word of caution: blind analysis of a child's artwork is dangerous. It is imperative to have the child actively explain the meaning of the picture (Thompson and Allan, 1985). The drawings must be viewed in the gestalt, especially when trying to grasp symbolic meaning. Nothing is universal. Therefore, to see something as only an isolated part and not related to the whole is dangerous (Naumburg, 1966; Rubin, 1978). Rubin states, "What makes more sense to me is to be aware of such common relationships, to have them available as hypotheses, but to remain open to other possibilities" (p. 66).

With this understanding, the following color preferences and symbols are offered as possible helpful guides.

Color

Color preferences change with age. Young children prefer the warm tones of red and yellow, while older children lean toward the cool colors of blue and green, with yellow becoming less and less preferable. Red remains a dominant color throughout all stages of life (Birren, 1969, 1978; Pasto, 1968).

It is not the colors per se that are important, but the context in which they are used within the drawing. Abnormal or excessive use of color or color combinations help give greater insight into the child's emotional state.

Conventional Uses of Color. Red is commonly used for

chimneys, lips, hair, cherries, and apples; orange for sweaters and oranges; yellow for flowers and the sun; green for female clothes, sweaters, roofs, grass, and trees; blue for the sky, clothing, eyes, and curtains; purple for women's clothing; black for smoke, outlining main parts, hair, shoes, belts, and doors; brown for hair, clothes, eyes, tree trunks and branches, and walls; white for fences and clouds (Buck, 1978; Jolles, 1957).

Unconventional Use of Color. Red is the most emotional color. It can show impulsiveness and spontaneity of expression (Cooper, 1978; Pasto, 1968; Zimmerman and Garfunkel, 1942), a need for affection from a significant person, or a sign of aggression and hate if used heavily (Alschuler and Hattwick, 1943; Birren, 1969; Jolles, 1957). It may also signify martyrdom (Cooper, 1978).

Orange is seen as red with greater emotional control, showing sympathy and friendliness (Alschuler and Hattwick, 1943; Birren, 1969) or an indication of aggressive resistance to dependency (Pasto, 1968).

Yellow, like red, can indicate spontaneous expression (Zimmerman and Garfunkel, 1942) or aggressiveness and hostility if overemphasized (Alschuler and Hattwick, 1943; Birren, 1969; Brink, 1944), even to the point of violent self-destruction (Pasto, 1968). For Cooper (1978), yellow is an ambivalent color. If golden or light yellow, it represents intellect, intuition, faith, and goodness. If dark yellow, it signifies treachery, jealousy, ambition, secrecy, and faithlessness.

Green may point to an escape from anxiety, a sense of controlled behavior, a return to an untroubled nature. Overall, the emphasis indicates no strong underlying emotional core (Alschuler and Hattwick, 1943; Birren, 1969; Kadis, 1950; Pasto, 1968).

Blue usually indicates an introverted person who has conscious emotional control. If done heavily, it represents a need for self-control (Alschuler and Hattwick, 1943; Birren, 1969; Jolles, 1957; Kadis, 1950; Pasto, 1968). Cooper (1978) believes that blue represents truth, intellect, wisdom, constancy, prudence, peace, contemplation, and the feminine principle symbolized by water.

Purple evinces a strong power drive almost bordering on paranoia. This is due in part, perhaps, to the fact that purple is the royal color (Buck, 1978; Pasto, 1968).

Black and brown represent inhibitions, repression, and depression with possible regression if used sloppily (Alschuler and Hattwick, 1943, 1969; Bieber and Herkimer, 1948; Brink, 1944; Cooper, 1978; Napoli, 1946; Pasto, 1968; Precker, 1950).

White has two opposing symbolic meanings. For Jolles (1957), white connotes anti-social attitudes, while Cooper (1978) believes that white symbolizes transcendence, simplicity, perfection, and purity.

Summary of Color

It is our experience that these interpretations of color have been frequently reliable. However, another word of caution: with children there are color fads. In the late 1970s, purple was the "in" color. So, to have interpreted an unusual amount of purple in a child's drawing during that period as indicating paranoia would have been questionable. Therefore, it is important to be aware of what the present-day children's fads are in colors.

Common Symbols of Children

It must be remembered that no symbol has a universal meaning. Any symbol has more than one meaning. How the symbol appears in the child's drawing in relation to the other parts of the drawing decides how the symbol is to be interpreted. Additionally, whether a symbol represents a positive or negative quality depends on how it is used in the picture and how it is assessed by the child. The child's cultural background is also critically important, as symbolic meanings vary in different cultures.

Apples represent fertility, love, joyousness, knowledge, wisdom, divination, or deceitfulness and death (Cooper, 1978; de Vries, 1976). Children usually use the apple to symbolize a need for emotional nurturance. When they draw worms in the apples and/or state that the apples are rotten, they are indicating that their nurturance has not been positive.

Birds represent transcendence: a "liberation from any state of being that is too immature, too fixed or final . . . any confining pattern of existence (to a) move toward a superior or more mature stage of development" (Jung, 1964, p. 149). Birds can also symbolize the soul or the soul's ascent to heaven (Cooper, 1978; de Vries, 1976). In our experience, birds usually appear in children's drawings when they experience a transformation within themselves.

Cats have a variety of meanings. They can represent desire, liberty, and stealth. A black cat can connote evil and death, playfulness, and grace (Cooper, 1978; de Vries, 1976). For a child, a cat usually represents a pet in his or her life, often a focus for the child's affection or need for affection.

Clouds. The color is important. If white, they symbolize spiritualism and purity. If dark in color, they evidence depression, disgrace or lament, or represent blockers of truth and knowledge (Cooper, 1978; de Vries, 1976). If blue, they may mean tears and the need to cry.

Dogs. Like cats, dogs have contrasting meanings. They can symbolize fidelity, watchfulness, nobility, depravity, scavenging, or fury (de Vries, 1976). For a child, a dog usually has the same meaning as a cat, though it can represent a stronger instinctual side.

Fire symbolizes a renewal of life, transformation, purification, passion, impregnation, power, defense, protection, or destruction (de Vries, 1976). For a child, fire is commonly destructive and indicates hostility. But if associated with an explosion in nature— e.g., a volcano—it can represent a release of emotion and the possibility of a transformation to a renewal of life.

Fish may be phallic symbols. They may signify fecundity, procreation, or life renewed and sustained (Cooper, 1978; de Vries, 1976). While we have not been able to substantiate this interpretation in children's drawings, it has been boys nearing the end of their latency period who have drawn fish.

Horses can symbolize life and death, instinctual animal nature, dynamic power, nobility, or the intellect (Cooper, 1978; de Vries, 1976). Though, again, these interpretations in children's drawings are not substantiated, horses have been most common in the drawings of girls around age twelve. Due to the sexual development of many girls at this age, the horse could symbolize the awakening of their instinctual animal nature.

A *house* may represent any of the following: the child's family life and relationships, openness to outsiders, the degree of protection that it offers, nature of the present ego structure, contact with reality, the relative roles played by the psychological past and future in the child's psychological field, and the degree of rigidity in the personality (Buck, 1948, 1978).

A house without a chimney may indicate a child's inability to express his feelings in the family situation. If a great deal of smoke is emanating from the chimney, it indicates strong emotions within the family.

Latent hostility is suggested if the house is windowless (especially on the ground floor), has drawn curtains, or a door with heavy hinges and lock. Houses without ground floor windows may indicate something is being kept secret or not disclosed.

A house that is leaning indicates a loss of psychic equilibrium (Spencer, 1969). If the house is moving, it may imply mental illness (Buck, 1948, 1978).

The *moon* rarely appears in children's drawings. It is included here because it represents the opposite gender of the sun, and sometimes it indicates that things are happening in the night.

Mountains are the symbol of constancy, eternity, firmness, and stillness (Cooper, 1978; de Vries, 1976). Children who draw mountains and include them as a main item in their discussion of the drawing tend to support the interpretation of constancy or a need for something constant in their life.

People. A pictured person discloses how the child feels physically and emotionally at the moment, what he would like to be, and the general attitude toward interpersonal relationships. People do not have to represent the child; they can be significant others in the child's psychological environment (Buck, 1948, 1978).

Size is usually equated with power: the bigger, the stronger. When and where the person is drawn in relation to other figures signify the child's position and status in relation to those people. Force or action between people usually indicates rivalry and/or aggression (Burns and Kaufman, 1970; di Leo, 1970).

Missing or oversized facial parts represent a problem with reception of stimuli. Missing features indicate a denial of function, malfunction of the part(s), or a wish for less reception. If parts are enlarged, the disproportion reveals a bombardment or preoccupation with the function of those parts (Buck, 1948, 1978; Burns and Kaufman, 1970). A head that is decidedly small compared to the rest of the body evidences a disturbed, depressed person (di Leo, 1970).

Missing hands or feet indicate a child's feeling helpless or immobile, unable to escape the situation. Legs and feet facing in opposite directions can point to a feeling of frustration and a desire to abandon current circumstances. (With younger children, however, this is a normal position.) Feet that are small in comparison to the rest of the person imply an unstable personality, while accentuated hands and/or arms are evidence that the person exerts forceful or aggressive actions (di Leo, 1970). This can also be a symbolic indication of child abuse.

If the body has a target drawn on it, especially in the genital region, child abuse is a strong possibility.

Ocean or Water. These are the primordial waters which are the source of all life. They can represent life and death, and then regeneration, the sea of life which has to be crossed, or the chaos and formlessness in the present life of the child (Cooper, 1978; de Vries, 1976).

Rain has two broad symbolic meanings: fertility and spiritual revelation. The fertility aspect can be fecundity or penetration, while the spiritual aspect can be divine blessing, beatitude, or purification (Cooper, 1978; de Vries, 1976). When children use rain in their drawings, it commonly connotes sadness. Rain is usually present in pictures that feature a house and thus indicates that there is some problem for the child at home. A rainstorm indicates acute distress and tempestuous feelings.

151

Sun. In most cultures, the sun represents the masculine power, but in some others it signifies the feminine power instead (Cooper, 1978, p. 162). The sun can be a healer, restorer, source of wisdom and purity, or the inborn fire in man's libido. In children's drawings, the sun usually represents warmth and the provider of growth. It may represent the person in the child's life who supplies the warmth and understanding necessary for development. However, if the sun is setting, either depression or death in some form may be indicated. A rising sun is usually representative of birth and renewal. When the sun is totally in the "wrong" place (i.e., near the lower righthand corner of the page), it may indicate a severely impaired father–child relationship (i.e., one where abuse and seduction are occurring).

A *tree* appears to represent five aspects of the child's psyche: the unconscious picture of the general psychological field, the unconscious developmental picture, the psychosexual level and maturity, contact with reality, and feelings of intrapersonal balance. Drawing a tree supposedly stimulates associations concerning the child's life role and ability to derive satisfactions in and from his environment in general (Buck, 1948, 1978).

A tree's lines that flow upward from a strong base but not outward indicate that the inner self goes from basic reality to emotional unreality.

If the tree is dead, it represents the psychological feeling of the child. Dead branches may portray environmental trauma, perhaps the loss of a loved one (Bluestein, 1978).

Branches reaching for the sun show a deep need for affection. If the top of the tree bleeds off the top of the paper, the child is prone to escape to fantasy for satisfaction and to avoid reality.

A tree leaning in the direction of the child's drawing hand shows a longing for control over his or her self-being or trying to escape from the dominant person pictured in the drawing. Leaning in the opposite direction suggests a longing for things to be as they were in the past. A moving tree is usually associated with a violent force being applied to it from the environment (Buck, 1948, 1978).

The trunk is a basic view of the child's psychological strength. A broken trunk shows a deep trauma within the child. If it is scarred or has bent, broken, or dead branches, a psychological trauma has usually occurred sometime in the past. The position of the damage on the trunk is supposedly proportional to the child's age when the trauma occurred. If the trunk appears not to be attached or to be disassociated from the canopy, it is a strong indication of intrapersonal conflict.

Part II

Fantasy and Drama

Chapter 8

FANTASY ENACTMENT IN THE TREATMENT OF A PSYCHOTIC CHILD

IN THIS PAPER we describe the therapy of a psychotic child. When Luci was referred to our clinic at age five and one-half, she had already been assessed by a number of professionals. Reports from them and her mother indicated that Luci had been a very passive baby who at twenty-three months still had no words and made only inarticulate noises. Luci did not respond to people and played alone, fascinated with her own fingers or toes. It appeared that she ignored speech and was locked into her own inner world. As Luci grew older her speech developed but other behavior deteriorated. She continued to operate at a very primitive, labile emotional level. The early diagnosis had been infantile autism, yet by the age of five she could be more accurately described as suffering from childhood schizophrenia because of her rich and bizarre fantasy life.

Behavior at the Start of Treatment

At the start of treatment Luci's behavior reflected confused identity, violence, and avoidance behavior toward people. She entered the therapy sessions in a highly animalistic state and tore off most of her clothing. She would become a raving dog, crawl about on the floor, barking and tearing at the therapist's legs, while at other times Luci would become a seagull in flight, screeching and flapping her arms. As the sessions progressed, Luci began insisting that she was a boy. For example, she would say: "I am a boy. Look at the hair on my face, chest and arms. I shave, feel my muscles. Don't call me Luci. I'm not Luci."

Luci resorted to these behaviors during times of stress and fear. These occurred repeatedly throughout the day. In fact, Luci was afraid most of the time. During such episodes, it was impossible for her to extricate herself from the role. She would persist in her identification despite reasoning to the contrary. If, for example, someone were to hold her hand, she would say, "How do you like my fluffy white wing," or "Hi, my name is Danny."

When adults approached Luci, she would deny her own identity and avoid contact by reverting to a bizarre posture, thus effectively cutting off relating and communication. When she saw babies in their mothers' arms, she would viciously attack the infants. Luci, on a deeper level, was unable to show love; she never kissed her parents or sat on their laps and refused to allow anyone to touch her or to give her love. Whether at home or in the therapy room, despite much encouragement, she never played with any toys except in a repetitive and manneristic fashion. In short, she remained locked into an egocentric stage of development which excluded any external attachments.

It was for this reason that traditional play therapy with toys did not appear to be an effective method of treatment. As Luci was best able to relate in the guise of different identities, we decided to remove the toys from the playroom and follow her through the fantasy world which she freely constructed. In other words, rather than denying these fantasies, we, ourselves, participated in their enactment and assumed the roles she assigned to us. We attempted to make tangible some of the inner world sensations and thus validate the reality she was experiencing. Drawing and painting were encouraged both at the end of the therapy session and at home.

Sixty-minute sessions were held on a weekly basis in a play therapy room. Both a male and a female therapist worked together with Luci over a period of a year. Luci's mother was also seen weekly by the male therapist for supportive counseling.

Behavior during the Enactment of Fantasies

In these sessions, Luci adopted a variety of different identities and rearranged the room in accordance with the themes that emerged. Over time it became apparent that these fantasy identities and settings enabled her to get in touch with a number of significant emotions and to give expression to distinct feeling states, particularly (1) rage, (2) depression, (3) anxiety and fear, (4) dependency, and (5) individuation.

The techniques adopted involved letting Luci initiate the fantasies or dramas and providing the structure to free her from psychotic perseveration when this occurred.

1. Rage

In the opening session, Luci reversed all of the "actors'" genders. She became Danny, the female therapist became Lawrence, and the male Joanna. She described Danny as the "little person" and Joanna and Lawrence as the "big people." In this drama, "Danny" tied up and attacked the two "big people." In a methodical and thorough manner, "Danny" pretended to cut our hair, clothing, our limbs, and finally our necks. Luci continued to attack us for the rest of the session even though we were lying "dead" on the floor. The feelings were so strong that she continued the onslaught for the next forty-five minutes with us pretend screaming and pleading for mercy. Finally, as she was unable to stop herself, we dragged ourselves to the other end of the room where we erected an "invisible shield" and became our true selves once more. For a while Luci insisted she was "Danny" and continued to attack the shield. However, after ten minutes of our refusing to enter into Luci's fantasy, she came behind the shield and sat quietly on our laps.

When Luci joined us behind the "shield," we briefly reviewed the main aspects of the sessions. For example, we said: "Danny really wanted to hurt Lawrence and Joanna today; he really wanted to cut them up, didn't he, and he couldn't stop himself, could he? He

159

just kept on cutting their hair, their hands, their legs, their necks, over and over again. I guess Danny feels he's been hurt a lot by the 'big people' and now he wants to do some hurting. I guess, Luci, when you were a little girl, you felt that the 'big people' were hurting you a lot."

The rage continued to pour out in the next three to four sessions. "Danny's" blows were stronger and more painful, and even though there was a lot of our "blood" everywhere, "Danny" was still not satisfied. He repeatedly fired pins into our eyes, mouths, and sexual organs. Our bodies were lying in blood, and then worms appeared and began emerging out of our rotting limbs. Soon we were "floating in a sea of pooh and blood" and being made to eat the pooh while "Danny" sat above us on dry land eating "deluxe hamburgers and chips." We acted out the pain, the cries of woe, while Luci enacted the punishing role.

Again, when behind the "shield," we reflected the feelings that were expressed during the sessions: "Danny liked to hurt us, he wanted to see us rot and eat 'bad food.' I guess at one time he felt the 'big people' had given him some 'bad feelings.'"

It seemed to us that the reversed sexual identifications acted as a screen for Luci and enabled her to express very violent feelings of hate and rage which previously she had attempted to repress from consciousness. When these feelings emerged, Luci was completely overwhelmed by them and could not extricate herself from them. Hence, we had to employ the "shield" as a device for calming her down. Usually, she would try to tease us out from behind it for five or ten minutes before she was able to listen to our reflections of her feelings. This rage seemed to extinguish itself after about five sessions. At the end of this stage, we noticed that Luci's drawings moved from seagulls flying to people on the ground. The adults were large and she was small (figs. 8.1 and 8.2). A deep depression followed.

2. Depression

One day following this intense period of rage, Luci came into the therapy session in a very depressed state. She spoke only in a

FIG. 8.1   Luci and Mother

FIG. 8.2   Luci and her therapists

whisper and related a dream in which she had visited the "dead land." In this land there were "no people, no fires in the fireplaces, no food in the refrigerators, no beds in the bedrooms, and no furniture in the living rooms. Outside there are no flowers, no grass, only rocks." This deep depression stayed with her for about three weeks and persisted outside of the therapy room. She refused to talk at pre-school, was very lethargic and at home just lay on her bed.

During the dramatization of this dream sequence, we would reflect and verbalize the sensations she was now experiencing. For example, we would say: "Danny is very unhappy. There's nothing to eat, and it's cold and empty and he's all alone." When behind the "magic shield" we would talk more directly to her: "It must have been a very hard place for Danny to grow up in. . . . Luci, maybe you felt unhappy and lonely when you were a little girl."

As the depression slowly began to lift, Luci now started to divide the room into the "good and the dead place." She would move between the two and altered her mood and language to correspond with her location. In the good place, she became quite animated and imagined flying in an airplane accompanied by her mother to a warm, sunny place. Here, there was an abundance of good things. When back in the "dead place" she would turn out the lights, close the blinds, and lower her voice. As it was impossible to make the playroom itself very dark, Luci moved into an adjoining window-less washroom. This move signified the transition to the third stage.

3. Anxiety and Fear

In this dark washroom, referred to as "the pump room," Luci related a dream in which she would wake up in the middle of the night to find "monster pumps" under the bed, hovering in the air, squeezing her stomach and suffocating her (fig. 8.3).

In subsequent sessions in the "pump room," Luci re-enacted her dream, with us becoming the target of the pumps' attack. Luci controlled the pumps and directed them to all parts of our bodies. She would become a pump, clutching legs and necks and pretend-

FIG. 8.3   Pumps on my bed

ing to suffocate us as she felt the pumps had done to her. There were times when Luci was unable to contain her panic and attempted to hurt us. When this occurred, we took a more active role and firmly yet gently held her arms until the desire to hurt had passed.

In the early stages of the fear and anxiety phase, the feelings were so overwhelming that they persisted outside the therapy room. At home and at school Luci now adopted a "Supergirl" identity which was also reflected in her drawings. "Supergirl" was never afraid, she had huge bulging muscles (fig. 8.4), and in confrontations with the pumps always emerged the winner. It seemed to us that Luci's new identity represented her attempt to protect herself from constant fear. In her drawings, the pump monsters evolved from "pyramids" (fig. 8.5) to "pumpkin faces" (fig. 8.6) and finally to "people chasing" her (fig. 8.7).

As the sessions continued, Luci seemed to gain mastery over the pumps by redirecting them from herself to us. We became aware

163

FIG. 8.4   Supergirl

FIG. 8.5   Pyramids

FIG. 8.6   Pumpkin faces

FIG. 8.7   People chasing me

that the intensity of her fear was diminishing and that she was now deriving pleasure from our screaming with fear and pleading for the pumps to stop. In other words, the sensations she once experienced with great anxiety and fear were now a source of sadistic pleasure and power. The sadistic pump behavior continued for four or five sessions until we found ourselves becoming increasingly irritated by it. We now felt that Luci did not want to give up the pumps. It seemed to us that she was "locked into" these sadistic impulses. At this point we reflected Luci's obvious pleasure and our impression that she did not want to give them up: "Danny, you really like these pumps to attack and hurt us. You really like those hurting pumps and don't want them to go away." Luci smiled and continued with the pumps' attacks.

When it became apparent that the repeated reflection of feeling did not alter Luci's behavior, we began to verbalize our own growing feelings of annoyance and irritation: "Danny, we're getting angry with these pumps. We wish they would stop attacking us. We don't like it." However, the onslaught continued, so we set a limit: "Danny, if the pumps attack us once more, we're all going to leave the pump room for today."

Luci's response to the limit-setting was immediately to have the pumps attack us. We then left the pump room and terminated the session, telling Luci we would see her again next week.

In the next session, Luci immediately asked to go into the darkened pump room, which we did, and after a long silence we became conscious of a new sound. Luci had lowered her voice and with a gentle, swishing sound had introduced a "baby pump." This reflected a move to yet another phase.

4. Dependency

Following the voicing of our annoyance at the pumps' attacks, Luci's drawings at home began to show dramatic change. She no longer drew the "Supergirl," so characteristic of the fear stage. Her drawings began to reflect incubatory activity (figs. 8.8 and 8.9) and the emergence of a new "insect life" (fig. 8.10). This supported

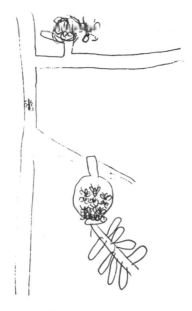

FIG. 8.8   Bee's nest

our impression that Luci was going through a transformation period out of which new feelings were evolving.

In the actual sessions Luci now insisted on bringing a blanket with which she covered our heads. With the greater security and darkness offered by this cover, Luci was able to sit comfortably on our laps for the first time. It was in this new setting that the "baby pump" emerged. When the "baby pump" appeared, Luci would whisper and coax the pump to join us.

At first the pump was very timid and scuttled back into the darkness when spoken to. When we were very quiet again, the "baby pump" re-emerged. Slowly, the "baby pump" was persuaded to stay with us longer and eventually sat on the palm of "Danny's" hand and allowed him to feed it. At this time, the "baby pump" would stay out for five or ten minutes before retreating. After the one incident of limit-setting mentioned above, the sadistic pumps did not appear.

FIG. 8.9   Chipmunks in trees

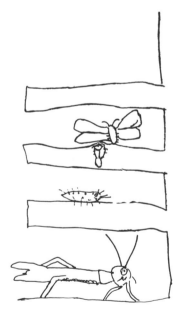

FIG. 8.10   Insects

Between sessions, Luci's drawings now revealed the natural evolution of the gestation period. She became fascinated by the birth process and began copying pictures of gestation (fig. 8.11), birth (fig. 8.12), severance of the umbilical cord (fig. 8.13) and breast feeding. At home, Luci began playing with dolls for the first time.

As the sessions progressed, the "baby pump" became part of the "family" (that is, Joanna, Lawrence, Danny, and "baby pump"). In response to Danny's direction, the family did everything together and several day-to-day patterns of family life were enacted. For example, at this stage, the baby pump would wake up with the family, have meals with the family, give good-night kisses and end the day by going to bed with them. (Figure 8.14 depicts her drawing of a family of puppies in bed.) This nurturant activity lasted four sessions.

Subsequent to these developments in the "pump room," nurturing behavior emerged at home. Luci now became very affectionate

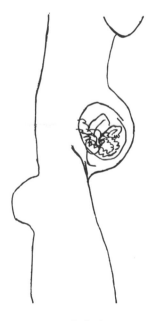

FIG. 8.11   Baby in tummy

169

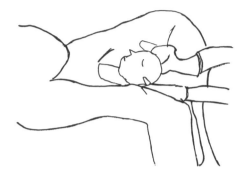

FIG. 8.12   Birth

FIG. 8.13   New baby

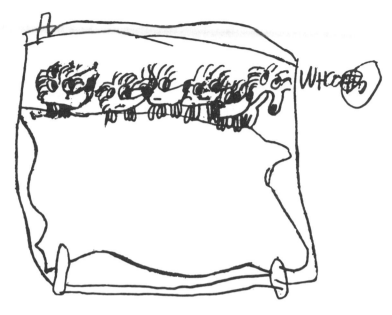

FIG. 8.14   Puppies in bed

with her mother, father and teacher and asked them to hold and kiss her. In addition, she became fascinated by babies and wanted to pick them up and cuddle them. At the same time, she began to play cooperatively with her brothers and other children.

5. Individuation

After four weeks of nurturant activities, Luci requested that we move from the pump room back into the therapy room. For the first time in this setting she showed an interest in toys. Luci no longer used the "Danny" identity and assumed her own name. In play therapy Luci used plastic figures and animals to continue her work on the themes of nurturance, intimacy and the control of aggression. Mother animals now protected their young, wild animals were corralled, and eventually a father figure appeared who tried to subdue and tame the wild animals. Her play therapy now assumed the characteristics of age-appropriate play, i.e.,

171

crafts, dolls and cowboys and Indians. She assumed the identity of an Indian Princess and often depicted herself riding back to camp (fig. 8.15) and cooking meat (fig. 8.16). On a symbolic level, cooking meat indicates that she could now use the heat of her aggression for constructive and nurturing processes.

Concurrent with this play stage, we moved Luci from our specialized pre-school program into a normal first-grade class. After an initial period of adjustment, Luci was soon able to cope with the work and enter into relationships with her teacher and classmates. Her progress was reflected in her continued mastery of tasks and ability to enjoy both spontaneous and structured activities with other children. As psychotic behavior did not reappear during the latter part of the school year (four months), we gradually terminated play therapy. One of her last drawings, the Indian Princess weeping, reflected her sadness in terminating and her new-found ability to weep.

Discussion

Stages in Luci's Therapy. Luci's therapy seemed to reflect a process in which her feelings were expressed, acknowledged and eventually mastered. At the start of treatment she denied all feelings except that of a pseudo-happiness. Even if pushed to tears, she would say, "My eyes are smiling, I'm always happy." When the anger did erupt it was never Luci who was angry, but a "raving dog." It seemed to us that the denial of all painful feelings resulted in her preoccupation with seagulls, feathers, balloons, and flight behavior. During play, Luci began to acknowledge and express her rage by using the identity of Danny. Following this, she relinquished the seagull behavior and became more grounded. But her drawings showed that she now felt very small and vulnerable while the adults appeared as "friendly giants."

After a lot of rage had been expressed, deep-seated feelings of depression emerged. Luci was now able to feel her inner sensations of loneliness, emptiness and desolation. At times it seemed to us that the rage had been a defense against her awareness of these sen-

FIG. 8.15   Riding to camp

FIG. 8.16   Cooking meat

sations. When we acknowledged the depression and let Luci know that experiencing it was necessary, the depression slowly lifted and new feelings emerged. The "dead land" eventually became both a good and bad place.

As new, positive feelings surfaced, Luci became very frightened and felt that she was being attacked. The experience of positive affect was alien to her and was hence perceived as threatening. The pumps were probably the symbol of this intrusive force. Lucy initially attempted to overcome her fear of intimacy and closeness by identifying with the attacking pumps and finally received sadistic pleasure from them.

It was only by our introducing a very firm limit that Luci could give up the sadistic component and allow herself to experience the intimacy and nurturance enacted in her care of the baby pump.

The therapy we have described above seems to reflect Fordham's (1966) concept of the deintegration of the primary self. The central aspect here is that deintegration eventually results in mother–child (therapist–Luci) symbiosis. This is a state of healthy intimate dependency. With Luci, this worked on two levels: she began to nurture the baby pump (herself), and she began to let others (parents, therapists, teachers) nurture her.

This symbiotic process seemed to lead to the birth of new feelings, manifested by images of incubation and insect life. These images paved the way to drawings of human gestation, birth separation and nurturance, leading to the start of her individuation process.

It seemed to us, then, that the fundamental changes occurred first within Luci. As they happened, Luci allowed her mother to approach her and for the first time was responsive to her mother's warmth and care. This represents a rather different view from that which is usually described in the literature, where the mother is seen as the primary cause of the disturbed behavior and consequently her growth is a precondition for growth in the child. There is no doubt in our minds that Luci was "an unusually difficult baby" (Allan, 1976) with a very rigid stimulus barrier surrounding the primary self, and that it was this which led to psychotic behavior and the disruption of attachment with the mother. In such cases, the focus of therapy should be on the child rather than the mother or family.

Theoretical Comparisons. It seemed to us that Luci could accurately be described as a primary autistic child (Anthony, 1958). During the first three years of life she failed to emerge from an initial withdrawn and autistic state. She was practically mute, seldom smiled at people, avoided eye contact, and played with objects in a repetitious and manneristic fashion. In Fordham's (1966) terminology, there would have been:

> a persistence of the primary self, an integrate which in healthy growth deintegrates to produce a symbiotic relation between the infant and mother. Since the integrate persists, no distinction can develop in the child between environment, ego, and internal world because these three entities are not distinguished but remain one whole self. (p. 299)

This occurred with Luci: there had been no deintegration of the primary self. For those first three years there had been an impenetrable barrier (Bergman and Escalona, 1949) around the primary self which prevented both deintegration and the establishment of relationships. Normal mothering practices failed to penetrate or change this barrier, and Luci remained locked into her own autistic inner world.

When Luci was three, a speech therapist told the mother she must actively stimulate speech by talking to her more and by demanding verbal responses. Normal speech patterns slowly emerged but tended to be interspersed between animal noises, echolalia, a rich fantasy life, and perseverative questioning. With the mother's persistent intrusion, between the ages of three to five years, Luci's primary self began to de-integrate, and as it did various emotions emerged—but with devastating force. During this stage, she moved from autism into psychosis. For example, when different feeling states erupted, Luci completely identified with them. The raw feelings took her over, and she became "a seagull in flight," "a boy called Danny," or "a raving dog." She had no defense against this. During the first three years of her life, the rigid "stimulus barrier" had prevented the energy of these feelings from being exposed, transformed, and regulated through normal parent–child interaction.

The findings that emerged in the course of Luci's first five years tend to contradict some of Bettelheim's (1967) postulations concerning the etiology of autism. He feels that autistic children often make rudimentary attempts to contact their environment but give up due to repeated frustration of their efforts to strive and master the world. In cases of autism, Bettelheim sees the parents as too controlling at too early a stage of the child's development, continually frustrating the child's own attempts at mastery of the environment. The child responds with rage and hatred. This affect is so overwhelming that it is repressed and projected on to the world and people around him. In the process, the child projects the whole of his assertiveness and is left with only flight or avoidance patterns of behavior.

While we agree with Bettelheim regarding the concepts of repression and projection, it has been our experience that many cases of psychosis arise when the parents *fail to interfere with and disturb an infant who persists in a state of primary self*—that is, a state of non-emergence and non-relating. This has practical treatment implications which differ from Bettelheim's, namely, that the treatment of autistic children requires some active therapeutic intervention to stop perseverative actions and fantasies.

Treatment for Bettelheim revolves around the therapist's and child-care workers' interacting and relating on the child's own terms. The child is provided with the opportunity to relate in the way that he wants to. One of the central aspects of this method is that nothing must be done against the child's wishes. For example, in discussing one child's treatment, he states:

> The first activity that brought her out of her total isolation was a chasing game in which the important thing was that she initiate all action and we had to passively, but with enjoyment, follow her lead. Above all, we were not permitted to touch her. (Bettelheim, 1967, p. 32)

While agreeing with Bettelheim on the importance of following the child's fantasies and actions, we would disagree on the degree of therapist involvement. We actively followed Luci's initiative and let ourselves do, up to a point, what she wanted us to. This, we found, greatly increased the transference and facilitated the exposure of Luci's repressed feelings. However, after forty to forty-five minutes of intense involvement, we did not hesitate to step in and set firm limits in the form of the "shield," if this was required. Indeed, limit-setting and firmness, including holding (Allan, 1986), became a crucial part of treatment. Luci needed our external controls in order that her ego could escape from the overwhelming affect released when we allowed her feelings free expression.

As each session drew to a close, we employed the "shield" to extricate Luci from her perseverative fantasy. This also provided a period of relaxation, a period of transition from the overwhelming feelings stirred up in the session. During this phase of treatment, we would review the session in terms of the feelings that were expressed (re: Danny) and make a few interpretations of the preceding drama. Interpretations were limited to this part of the hour and about how Luci must have felt as a little girl. This was a planned strategy, for it has been our experience that reflection of feeling and use of interpretation to elucidate unconscious processes are employed too frequently, with the effect of threatening and inhibiting growth. Our confining these types of statement to the latter part of the hour left Luci free to experience and evolve her own "inner dramas" without our intrusion or interruption. This controlled use of interpretation, coupled with extensive periods of play, differs directly in degree from that of Bettelheim (1967), Fordham (1966), and Klein (1955).

Chapter 9

CREATIVE DRAMA WITH ACTING-OUT SIXTH AND SEVENTH GRADERS

A COMMON PROBLEM facing an elementary school counselor is an overwhelming caseload. Referrals often increase dramatically in the sixth and seventh grades. Tanner (1970) has suggested that this may be due, in part, to the onset of puberty, with its tremendous physical and emotional changes in the body. Increased adrenalin and the release of sex hormones result in a surge of energy and sexual development. These changes are often manifested behaviorally in hyperactivity in the classroom, impulsiveness, aggressiveness, destructiveness, and primitive exhibitionism or narcissism.

In psychological terms, puberty is the age of identity crisis (Erikson, 1968). With bodily changes and physical growth spurts, a child's self-definition is forced to change. Often, this results in a poor self-concept or lack of self-definition. Over-aggressiveness can be seen as a compensatory mechanism to hide a basic fear of inadequacy and feelings of threat from the realities of the larger, outer world.

Some children react to these changes in a less noticeable but equally devastating way by withdrawal. They become social isolates, often nervous, timid and shy, and are frequently cast as scapegoats by the rest of the class.

Problem

The problem I was faced with, both as a school counselor and as a counselor trainer, was to devise a method whereby a counselor

178

could begin to work effectively with such large numbers of referrals.

Dinkmeyer and Muro (1971) have suggested that a useful approach in treating children of this age group is some form of activity group therapy. In activity group therapy, children are able, within certain limits, to do and say what they want, to run around and generally "burn off" a lot of excessive and destructive energy. The theory behind this is that, after such a period of free expression, it is easier for these children to establish their own controls over their behavior. With that, destructive behavior decreases and constructive group activity and play emerge.

While this approach has been successful in residential settings and mental health clinics, it is not readily transferable to a "normal" elementary school setting because of the lack of appropriate facilities and because of the disruptive effects it would have on the discipline of the school as a whole.

The problem, then, was that the treatment method—activity group therapy—had some merit, but that its traditional form of practice was not appropriate to the school setting.

Method

Faced with this dilemma, I decided to explore the use of a form of treatment that I have termed "Creative Drama." This method has some aspects of both activity group therapy and developmental drama as used by Spolin (1963), Way (1967) and Layman (1976). The rationale behind this approach stems from my observation that a central characteristic of the children referred for counseling was their high need to be noticed. That is, an inevitable consequence of their behavior was that they "stood out" in the classroom, everybody was forced to pay attention to them, and they were always "clowning or commanding the stage." It was decided, then, to legitimize this need by giving the children a clearly defined space and time where they could literally have the "full stage."

The purpose of this method was to remove from the classroom

for forty minutes a week the students who were "acting out," bring them together in groups of seven or eight each, and encourage them to "develop or create a drama or play," which would then be filmed on videotape and played back immediately afterward. The plays could be from their imagination, from TV or films, or any combination of the above.

I defined my role and those of three graduate student assistants as "facilitators," whose purpose was to help the children (a) talk out the plays they wanted to do, (b) select one, (c) share the roles, (d) carry out a short rehearsal, (e) perform the play for videotaping and (f) then discuss what they saw. In the discussion stage, we would focus on three questions: (a) "What did you like about to-day's drama?" (b) "What did you not like?" and (c) "What would make it better next time?"

As in activity group therapy, our goal was to let the children take most of the initiative for discussion of themes, developing a particular theme, preparation, and execution of the final drama. We were there to clarify what they were doing and to help them focus in order to accomplish the task. In this sense we tended to alternate between being non-directive and directive, depending on how their interactions with each other were progressing. If the drama was getting too elaborate or had bogged down, then the facilitator might clarify the issues, make some suggestions, and then back off to let the children take over again.

The children discussed setting limits and decided on two general rules:

1. No one must get physically hurt.
2. Everyone should try to listen when someone talks.

Objectives

We had a number of objectives in mind when we initiated this project. We tried to provide a space and emotional climate that allowed for:

1. burning off excessive energy;
2. expressing impulses and affects that are commonly felt at

this age but not normally allowed expression—narcissism, anger and power needs;

3. sharing the fantasies, images and themes that were uppermost in their minds.

Through this expression, it was hoped that the children would:

1. *Find it easier to regulate their aggressive impulses in their everyday lives.* We hoped that the expression of feeling in a therapeutically controlled environment would give them a much better chance to understand their feelings and to better exercise voluntary control over them.

2. *Be able to work cooperatively with other peers in a small group setting.* Having to "develop a play or drama" involves sharing ideas, listening to each other, and working together in a flexible way to get the task completed. These are all important small group skills which we thought the children could learn and then apply in the classroom and other life situations.

3. *Learn to understand themselves better.* We hoped they would learn more about themselves by seeing their actions on the video monitor and responding to the facilitators' questions about what they liked and did not like about their performance. We hoped also that they would learn from the comments of their peers and from our asking them, "What could you do to make it better next time?"

4. *Learn problem-solving skills.* Presenting the students with the question "What drama do you want to do today?" is, in essence, like forcing a problem situation on them. Within a limited time and space, they have to decide what they are going to do and how they are going to do it and then carry it out.

5. *Learn to accept responsibility for their actions.* The facilitators made it clear at the start that they were not there as disciplinarians but to help them develop and act out their dramas. We held them responsible for their actions. If the play did not materialize or deteriorated when in progress, that was their responsibility. We would help them look at what had caused the failure and would ask them what they could do to prevent its happening again.

6. *Have a chance to experience roles (and hence behaviors and*

feelings) that they might not normally assume. For example, the drama situations might allow for the overly aggressive child to play passive-submissive roles and the fearful child to "practice" assertive and aggressive roles in a safe setting.

Subjects

Thirty children were involved from one elementary school. Referrals were made by the teachers on the basis of disruptive classroom behavior. There were seventeen boys and thirteen girls in the sample. Children were seen in groups of seven or eight each with one facilitator. The two sixth-grade groups were mixed boys and girls, while the two seventh-grade groups were homogeneous until the last month of drama. Group composition was decided by the children. A trainee counselor or I worked with each group as a facilitator.

Results

As the sessions progressed, we became aware of different stages and the emergence of several specific themes. Though there was some overlap between the stages and themes, they will be reviewed separately here.

Developmental Stages

As the dramas progressed, they moved through certain stages: (a) chaos, (b) control and chaos, (c) control, and (d) flexibility. At first, the students could not work together, could not listen to each other, and could not come to any agreement over which play they would do or which part they would take. When they did finally put on the play, they forgot their words and did not stick to the roles, and the play disintegrated into a mad chase, a free-for-all fight or just narcissistic posturing.

After three or four sessions, however, more elaborate plots did develop and were maintained during the performance for two to three minutes before the play disintegrated into a chaotic brawl. In this stage (two to three months), the students could maintain a good quality dialogue and effective interaction before fighting occurred. The third stage (third to fifth months) was that of total control; the students stuck to their parts and executed them with precision in a tight performance with no disintegration. The fourth stage (fifth to seventh months) demonstrated flexibility. Here, there was effective working together with considerable creativity, spontaneity (ad-libbing) and humor in the plots.

Specific Psychological Themes

Throughout the seven months, a record was kept of each play and the central theme recorded. At the end of the year, we found these themes could be grouped under eight headings, as follows.

1. *Narcissism and Exhibitionism.* In the beginning, the students could not work together at all but only draw attention to themselves in the most gross and primitive ways possible. They were fascinated by the video-camera. During group discussions the girls would constantly turn around, wave at the camera, comb their hair in front of it, and literally put on a song-and-dance routine. The boys were equally fascinated but more blatantly exhibitionistic. They would stand in front of the camera and yell a very prolonged "Intro-du-cing . . . " but never had anything to introduce or follow it.

Two themes did develop out of this showing off: "Dirty Jokes" (done four times) and "Flashing" (done three times). At first, individuals told the jokes rather rapidly into the camera. Eventually, their jokes and dirty stories became more formalized, with the group sitting down in a row of chairs. The first person would say a few words, then stop, and the second would add more and so on down the line until the joke, song or story was over. During the jokes they would often swear and call each other "gay."

In incidences of "flashing," the boys took great delight in pretending to exhibit themselves in front of the camera. They would turn their rear-ends to the camera, pat their buttocks, ex-

183

pose the insides of their mouths and repeatedly give the "finger" gesture. The highlight came in a "flashing" sequence when, with encouragement from the other boys, one boy approached the camera with his jacket tightly wrapped around him, then stood in front of it, suddenly opening his jacket to expose a tee shirt with two large breasts printed on it. The other boys then rushed up and pretended to "feel and squeeze" the breasts to the delight of their peers.

As the dramas progressed, the exhibitionism and narcissism became sublimated and expressed in healthier ways. The flashing, crude language and giggling at the camera all but disappeared. As we became aware of their need for some form of narcissistic expression, we suggested that each time one member of the group should formally introduce to the camera the title of the play and the role taken by each member. At first the quality of their introductions was very poor. The presenter could scarcely look at the camera, and his word delivery would often be inaudible and too rapid. However, over time, face and eye contact to the camera improved, as did the verbal presentation of the plot. Toward the end of the sessions, more sophisticated forms of introduction evolved. For example, each actor would now be filmed during the introduction for a few seconds in an "action pose" that characterized his role in the play.

2. *Activity Themes.* Also during the first two months, a lot of time was spent just running around. An attempt was made to develop a theme, the children would do it for the camera, but it would end up in a mad chase. Out of this, the older seventh-grade boys devised two games: "Roller Derby" (done five times) and "Knee Hockey" (played three times). Roller Derby consisted of arranging gym mats in an oval shape and picking two teams who then ran around the track, tagging, bumping and trying to force each other off the mats. "Knee Hockey" was hockey played on the knees, without sticks and with a ball that was thrown as hard as possible toward the goalies.

Both games were played by the older boys only and resulted in many arguments (since they continually violated their own rules) and in "burning off" vast amounts of energy. The end effect was total exhaustion, all of them piled on top of each other on the floor.

These two themes, narcissism and physical activity, seemed to extinguish themselves over a period of two months and led into themes of oral aggression and dominance.

3. *Oral-Aggressive Themes.* There were two distinct types of drama here. The sixth graders devised plays that centered around "monsters" such as Dracula, Vampire, Sasquatch and "Jaws" (seven times), while the seventh graders performed plays that occurred in "bars" (eight times). The monster themes usually involved people out walking in a wood or swimming in the sea, who get attacked, bitten or eaten by the monster. Friends come to the rescue with the aid of crosses or stakes. The police are called in, and after a fight the monster is killed.

The bar scenes consisted of buying drinks, getting drunk, then acting and walking around drunk, refusing to pay for drinks, trying to pick up girls and getting into fights with the bartenders or other customers. The police would arrive, another fight would develop, and the "drunks" would be taken off to jail.

Toward the end of this phase, the themes became more original and showed elements of combining the two types of play. For example, four men get very drunk in a bar, and another man comes in and is asked to join the party. This man turns out to be Dracula, who slowly disposes of them one-by-one when they visit the washroom.

4. *Dominance Themes.* We became aware that dominance was clearly the students' favorite theme. At first, there were no plots, just everyone vying for the "tough guy" role, but over time three distinct plays emerged. Two of these were adapted from popular TV programs ("Happy Days," seven times, and "Bionic Man," three times), and one play they devised themselves ("Super-Chap," twice). The execution of these plays was usually well-controlled.

Though the plots varied, the theme was the same: "Might is right." The tough youth controlled the group; the tough man defeated monsters and criminals. In their plays, the main character to emerge was the "Fonz" from "Happy Days." The "Fonz" was the undisputed leader of the teenager gang. He snapped his fingers

185

and the gang jumped to attention or fell in line, with the pecking order clearly delineated. They did whatever he asked even when they had no wish to. When the "Fonz" played tricks on them, they did not challenge him but submitted weakly. They tried to identify with him by imitating his body mannerisms, his sayings and his clothes. But as the plays progressed, the "Fonz" became softer and was given the roles of mediator and problem-solver for intra-gang fights rather than that of autocratic boss.

The resolution of the dominance theme was seen in some of the last plays the students created. One in particular was called "Lazy Workers." Here, the boss gets mad at the workers for being lazy and a fight starts. Before the first blow is struck, there is a cut for an anti-perspirant commercial. When the commercial ends, the camera moves back to the fight, which is quickly over. The final shot is of the workers sitting on the boss.

5. *Moral Themes*. These themes all involved a highly organized plot (often taken from TV serials) that dealt with the struggle between "right" and "wrong." The emphasis was "Morality is right." Aggression was expressed but occurred at the end of the play and took second place to the plot. The plots were usually the same: planning a bank robbery, carrying it out, setting off the alarm. When the police move in, there is a chase and the police capture the robbers. The specific themes were bank robberies (seven), muggings (five), gang wars (three), and S.W.A.T. (three).

Unlike in the dominance plays, the power and hence the roles were equally distributed amongst seven or eight players. Each had an important and crucial part to play. A lot more emphasis was given here on the group effort (everyone working together) and precision. The timing had to be perfect, and retakes were made if something went wrong.

6. *Social Themes*. These themes were enacted by the older seventh-grade girls and included family fights (three times), running away from home (three times), shoplifting (twice), teacher-student conflicts (twice), vandalism (twice) and "Bully Girl" (once). The themes involved feelings of emerging independence and conflict with authority figures. The issue frequently was "You want us to do things your way but we want to do them our way."

186

Often a fight broke out, involving yelling, pretend slapping and running away. Sometimes the expression of anger occurred through vandalism and shoplifting. The outcome of these dramas was often that the girls were rejected by the authority figures for their "bad" behavior.

The moral and social themes seemed to give way in the last six weeks to two others: comedy and dance.

7. *Comedy.* As the year progressed, the dramas became more spontaneous and humorous until eventually the main theme was comedy (seven times). For example, with the sixth-grade boys, their final drama involved a group of pirates rowing to Treasure Island, who then get into a fight about how to share the spoils. The boat tips over and they all end up in the water. Then, one of them notices "Jaws" swimming slowly toward them. They panic until someone decides to give "Jaws" a flask of wine. This calms "Jaws" a little but not enough; the others reluctantly give "Jaws" all their wine, which makes him very drunk. They capture him, take him back to the Vancouver Aquarium, put him on display and charge admission.

Other dramas involved ethnic grocery-store jokes, psychiatrist jokes, classroom jokes and role-reversal situations. These plays were fluid and yet sophisticated, some of them having humorous "commercial" breaks at points of "high drama" (i.e., when someone was about to be knocked out).

In the last month, the seventh-grade boys and girls began to put on plays together. They worked on one of these for two sessions, with a plot centered on a role-reversal situation: two young men are walking home drunk from the beer parlor and are assaulted and beaten up by a gang of girls. They crawl home and are about to call the police when they get a threatening, anonymous telephone call (from the girls) saying: "You will be murdered at midnight." They call the local police who come over, find the story highly unbelievable, and take the two men to a psychiatrist's office where he administers the word association test to them.

There were a number of interesting features about this drama: (a) it represented the first time the boys and girls worked together as a large group (six boys and eight girls); (b) the boys allowed themselves to assume a passive role in relation to the girls, who enacted a very aggressive role; (c) the police were no longer cast as brutal and aggressive but were seen as friendly, humorous yet concerned people.

8. *Rhythmical Themes.* The last themes were scenes where the children imitated rock and roll concerts (twice) and a song and dance routine (once). For the sixth graders, there was some mixing of the sexes, though the girls tended to do the singing "on stage" while the boys formed part of the audience. The seventh graders developed a far more elaborate "song and dance" number. One song, "Saturday Night," was taken from the popular rock group "Bay City Rollers" and put to a dance routine. Both boys and girls formed the chorus line, and another group of boys and girls made up the rhythm section—improvising by clapping their hands and by stamping their feet in time. It was interesting for us to observe that the group asked the previously very shy and overweight girl to do the formal introduction of this number. She did it very well and then rejoined the group as part of the rhythm section.

This was their last time to do drama, and the children left feeling good about what they had done, sad that it was over and asking whether they could come again next year.

Table 2 below summarizes the themes, their approximate duration and frequency.

TABLE 2

Summary of Duration and Frequency of Drama Themes

	Theme	Duration	Frequency
1.	Narcissism and Exhibitionism	First month	7
2.	Activity	First–second months	8
3.	Oral-Aggressive	First–third months	15
4.	Dominance	Second–fourth months	12
5.	Moral	Second–fifth months	18
6.	Social	Third–sixth months	13
7.	Comedy	Fifth–seventh months	7
8.	Rhythmical	Seventh month	3

Evaluation

In order to assess the impact of the creative drama on the children, we waited for two months before administering an evaluation form to them. The rationale for this was that, if drama was effective in bringing about any deeper changes, these would still be remembered two months later; if the changes were superficial, not much credibility would be given to the sessions.

An evaluation form was designed to tap the children's thoughts and feelings about drama by asking them specific "yes" or "no" questions and by allowing them the opportunity to write in their own statements. The form was administered to twenty-six students (four having moved from the school following termination of drama). The results are presented below.

1. *Individual "Yes" or "No" Items*
   100% enjoyed the drama (26)
   100% felt the dramas improved as the year progressed (26)
   88% would have liked more discussion after the dramas (23)
   85% would like to come to drama again next year (22)
   85% thought drama helped them get along better in school (22)
   77% felt a lot better after drama (20)
   69% thought drama was one of the best things they have done in school (18)
   65% thought drama helped them understand themselves better (17)
   35% felt drama was a good way of getting out of class (9)
   27% thought they did not learn anything from drama (7)
   23% were upset about having to do extra work to catch up after drama (6)
   12% found it hard to go to class after drama (3)

As can be seen, all of the students enjoyed the drama sessions and felt they improved as the year progressed. Most (eighty-eight percent) would have liked more discussion after the dramas, and

189

eighty-five percent said they would like to be involved again next year. They felt drama helped them with their psycho-social development: twenty-two felt drama helped them get on a lot better in school, twenty felt a lot better after drama and seventeen thought drama helped them understand themselves. Eighteen children believed drama was one of the best things they have done in school, while nine students saw it as a good way of getting out of class. Seven felt they learnt nothing from drama, six did not like doing the extra work to catch up in their regular class afterward and three found it hard to work on returning to their class.

2. *Favorite Types of Drama*
   58% preferred dramas they made up themselves (15)
   42% preferred dramas based on TV themes (11)

Dramas based on TV themes were certainly popular at first. It was only with developing success and confidence that they started devising their own plays. Even at the end, the boys' favorite play was TV's "Happy Days," while for the girls it was the "Muggers and the Psychiatrist." Interestingly, both of these plays centered around the dominance theme. In "Happy Days," this theme emerged through the identification with the "Fonz," and in the "Muggers" the girls enacted a role-reversal situation in which they clearly dominated the boys.

3. *Directing and Playing the Parts They Wanted*
   65% said this occurred "sometimes" (17)
   19% said this "never" happened (5)
   15% said this "always" happened (4)

Most children thought they had some chance to play and direct the parts they wanted. Only five children felt they were never given this opportunity. In regard to group composition, twenty-nine percent wanted more "mixed boys and girls" and only one student wanted "boys only."

4. *Suggestions for Improvement*
   58% wanted the dramas left as they were (15)
   23% wanted more direction from adults (6)
   19% wanted no adult helpers (5)

Other suggestions included longer time, use of "real people," more discipline and better listening to each other. Most students seemed quite content with the drama left the way it was. Some students (six) found it hard to adjust to the style of the facilitators, while a few students (five) wanted total freedom with no adults present.

5. *Facilitators' and Teachers' Evaluation*

We were pleased with the outcome of the drama project. On the whole we felt our objectives were met. The children learned to work with each other in small groups—to listen, to develop and carry out a project, and to assume responsibility for their actions. The children also seemed to learn to channel their energy away from destructiveness into creativity and to allow themselves to experience roles that they would not normally assume. In addition, it seemed that the period of free expression (i.e., the phase of narcissism, exhibitionism and activity) did subside, resulting in the students' having much greater voluntary control over their destructive and immature impulses.

We had hoped for more application from the drama group back to the classroom, but only a few positive changes were noticed by the teachers. They were aware that students enjoyed the drama and that most seemed relaxed afterward. A few students, however, returned to the class quite hyperactive and disruptive. Certainly, more work needs to be done on this phase (see the *Conclusions and Implications* section below). However, it has been my experience that it takes time for the changes that occur in the psychotherapy of early adolescents to generalize out of the therapeutic setting (i.e., the drama room) into the classroom. Two boys with whom I worked several years ago have published a book (Mildiner and House, 1975) describing, in part, the important role that creative drama played in their psychological development.

Discussion

In this project we attempted to use the format of creative drama as a vehicle for providing counseling for a large number of sixth- and seventh-grade students. The method relied on the use of a group (seven or eight) of children to solve a problem (i.e., devise and act out a drama within a thirty-minute period) in the presence of facilitators and video equipment.

Counseling and psychological growth occurred for the students on an indirect level through involvement with their peers on a project. The drama allowed them to deal on a symbolic level, without too much cognitive awareness, with certain unresolved developmental and psychological issues, revolving around hyperactivity, poor frustration tolerance, narcissism, exhibitionism, oral-aggressive impulses, feelings of inferiority, poor ego identity and social concerns. Through their plays they dealt with these issues and developed more positive self-images.

Though I was aware of these underlying psychological issues, I did not verbalize or interpret them. The reason for this was that, by allowing the children to present and deal with their own fantasies and dramas, psychological evolution and growth would occur. It has been my experience that confrontations and interpretations can threaten a child's ego, often damaging the self-healing potential that lies within each child. This issue has been dealt with in more depth elsewhere (Allan and MacDonald, 1975).

In essence, we kept our input focused on the task of constructing the drama. We expected that the students would and could carry out this project. We clarified conflicts between them at times, trying to represent both points of view but leaving the decision to the group. In the discussion phase we provided the focus once again—"What did you like?" "What did you not like?" "What would make it better next time?"—but got them to do the evaluation. Occasionally, if there was time, we would ask them to explore their feelings within the role: "What was it like when you were mugged by the girls?" "When you got drunk?" "When the police came?" "When the mother hit the daughter?" "When Dracula bit you?"

The videotape proved to be an excellent source of feedback. Almost immediately we noticed that the children loved to be filmed and to see themselves on the monitor, observing and commenting on what they saw. Often they criticized or praised each other.

Stages and Themes. The outstanding characteristic of the drama was the evolution that occurred in both the stages and the themes, discussed here in terms of both Freudian and Piagetian frameworks.

It is well-known that in the puberty period there is a tremendous increase in libidinal energy and a re-activation of the intra-psychic struggle between the id, ego and super-ego (A. Freud, 1948). When the id gains the dominant position in this struggle, behavior greatly deteriorates. In Freudian terms, the behavior we observed in the regressive (or chaotic) phase would be called pre-oedipal: the gross-motor activity, the narcissism and exhibitionism, and the concern with orality (i.e., drinking and Dracula plays). Our giving the children the freedom of choice (i.e., letting them do the plays they wanted to do) seems to have enabled them to express and rework some unresolved issues from earlier developmental stages.

This "return" to an earlier developmental level is common in early adolescence generally (Offer, 1969). It is just that we used the regression therapeutically by clearly defining the space and time where it could take place. Wallace (1973) has commented on the importance of providing clearly defined protective boundaries (a "temenos") in which regression can occur. It is my experience that the failure to provide such a controlled space results in chaos and destruction with no inner, psychological growth. These boundaries would include preparation for entry into "emotional" time, submergence in "emotional" time, and preparation for re-entry into "ordinary" time. In our case, "emotional" time would be the drama sessions and "ordinary" time the classroom situation. Preparation for entry would be the warm-up discussions as to

193

what play to do, and preparation for re-entry would be the review and discussion of the video at the end of the drama session.

Also, by allowing regression within the context of drama, and with adults present, we probably compacted and shortened the period of regressive play. This enabled the students to move on to other psychological themes. It should be emphasized that we did not encourage or promote regression. We gave the children the freedom to do the dramas they wanted. It seemed to us that this group of "acting out" children needed to rework those particular themes and hence went directly to them. When I have done creative drama in "normal" classrooms, I did not experience this degree of regression; rather, the children acted out social issues (dominance themes, family and teacher issues, and boy–girl conflicts) and comedy.

The struggle between dependence and independence is another central theme of adolescence and one that becomes re-activated in puberty. From a Freudian point of view, the issue of dependence versus independence reflects a child's need to break his or her emotional ties with the mother. The child is tied to his or her mother by a need for nurturance, and independence occurs when he can break some of this reliance on the mother and find healthier ways of self-nurturing. We saw this particularly in the plays that centered around "bars" and "Dracula." These plays embodied the conflict between oral dependency (drinking) and the fear of psychological annihilation that comes from perpetuating this dependency for too long (symbolized by the threat of Dracula). On another level, we can see the struggle here between the id ("getting drunk in the bars") on one side and the super-ego on the other ("the police taking them off to jail").

We believe the dramas enabled the children to work and rework this theme symbolically until the issue was more or less resolved. Pretending to be drunk and walking in a drunk fashion let them work out some oral needs and enabled them to move on to another developmental stage. This movement occurred slowly over time (one to two months) and was seen in the second phase where the dramas were controlled at the beginning (when they played their drunk parts well) but disintegrated into chaos at the end (when the police came to arrest them and a disorganized fight followed).

In the third phase, that of control, the students were dealing with other adolescent themes—those of ego identity, peer group relations and the establishment of dominance–submission hierarchies. In the early phases of these dramas, the emphasis was on dominance and "grabbing" leadership. They all wanted to play the "Fonz." At first, it was hard to get them to develop a plot because they were all vying for the leadership role. Slowly, clear-cut hierarchical positions developed, based on strength; once this structure was established, the group started to work effectively as a whole. Each member of the group or "gang" had a role to play, but the parts were clearly not equal: the weaker members played only walk-on parts, while the "Fonz" dominated the action. Hartup (1970) has observed that children quickly develop dominance–submission hierarchies in whatever group they find themselves.

The dominance themes led to aggressive plays which emphasized another adolescent theme—that of moral development. These were plays of "cops and robbers"—the struggle between "good and bad" and "right and wrong"—with the good clearly winning. Here, every member of the group had an equally important part. There was no "key" figure; all were equally strong or equally criminal. Their ego identities appeared well-formed, and they functioned in the drama effectively and independently.

In these two themes, the underlying psychological issues seemed to center around the development of the ego (as exemplified by the hero figure, the "Fonz") and the integration of the ego and super-ego (the "good guys" and the "cops" became very concerned with "fighting crime"). In the dominance themes, the weaker members of the hierarchy developed their ego strength through identification with the "Fonz," as his admirers or sidekicks. In the moral themes, the children saw each other as equals. There were no incidences of regression or chaos in these themes, reflecting perhaps regulation and control of the id by the ego and super-ego and the development of individual ego identities.

At first, when we observed the older girls' group, we thought that, unlike the boys, they were not interested in dominance themes but rather social issues. However, on closer inspection, we became aware that there were strong dominance issues underlying the social dramas they were enacting, but that these were not as obvious as the boys'. For example, in the shoplifting scene we noticed that (a) the girl shoplifter so terrified the store manager that she let her off, (b) the "bully" girl on the playground ruined the other girls' games, and (c) in the "mugging" scene, the girls assumed the dominant position over the boys. This "covert" concern with power by girls has been observed by other researchers (Sutton-Smith and Savasta, 1972) and corrects the earlier belief that girls are not interested in power hierarchies.

The moral development issue received further elaboration in the girls' social dramas. Here, the struggle between right and wrong, dependence and independence was depicted from real-life scenes of the family and school. It was an "us against them" situation: "We are right. We know what is best for us, and we can manage on our own without parents or teachers."

Piaget (1948) attributed this "captivation-by-the-ideal" to the adolescents' new-found capacity for abstraction, which tends to result in a preoccupation with moral issues and a premature sense of autonomy.

The last phase was characterized by flexibility, spontaneity, and humor. The boys and girls now worked together in one large group. It seemed, however, that the separation by the seventh graders into gender-homogeneous groups for the first six months allowed them to solidify their own ego identities, and from that position of strength they could then begin to relate effectively to members of the opposite sex.

In the last phase, for both groups of boys and girls, the ego gained ascendency over the id and the super-ego. Flexibility and spontaneity were seen in the role-reversals, the humor and the ad-libbing. The students could allow themselves to experiment with roles and behaviors that they normally would not show (e.g., the boys allowing themselves to be beaten up, sat on, made fun of, and the girls dominating them). They were able to act freely without fear of the chaos caused by the id running amok. Even the police in these dramas were friendly, humorous people (not stereotyped character representations), who acted somewhat unconventionally. The last drama—the song and dance routine from the Bay City Rollers' Saturday Night theme—reflected the group's strength in a demonstration of physical closeness and intimacy (through dancing) before disbanding. Termination of early adolescent groups is usually difficult and, if the preparation has not been done, the last session is usually a non-session or a disaster.

In sum, if we look at the above phases from a Piagetian viewpoint, it seems that in a microcosm the students evolved through the three stages of moral development as delineated by Kohlberg (1970). The preconventional stage, where personal gratification and "doing what one can get away with" have priority, was seen in the chaotic or regressive phase. The conventional stage, accepting society's standards, was seen in the control phase, and the postconventional stage, the development of personal principles and standards, was evident in the flexible and humorous phase.

This does not mean that these students have resolved the problems of adolescence. Kramer (1968) has shown that regression and re-integration at a higher developmental level constitutes a common pattern in and of itself. It does mean, though, that these children have had a successful experience at several developmental stages and because of this will probably be able to cope with the other developmental tasks of adolescence. As can be seen from their evaluations, the experience seemed to be meaningful to them.

Conclusions and Implications

Several conclusions and implications can be drawn from this study. Creative drama is:

1. Popular with early adolescent children who have a high need for attention and are usually difficult to treat by other methods.

2. Perceived by these children as helping them get along better in school and understand themselves better.

3. A useful technique whereby one counselor can work with six to eight acting-out children at one time.

4. A method whereby students can enact fantasies and issues that are of concern to them and one which helps them develop the ability to work together in small groups.

5. More effective as a self-learning device when videotaped. The opportunity to see oneself in action provides a non-threatening means for self- and peer-evaluation.

Counselors using the creative drama approach must:

1. Be able to tolerate considerable anxiety and confusion when the students enter the regressive phase and believe that they will eventually be able to work their way through it to a more mature developmental level.

2. Ensure that they have a "protected" area for the drama sessions. This means that the noise from the sessions must not disrupt other school activities and that other children do not "break into" the drama sessions.

3. Devise appropriate methods for re-entry of the drama students back into the classroom. This was an area of weakness in the present study. It became apparent to us that forty minutes is too short for drama: it does not allow enough time for discussion or for relaxation for the students to make the transition back into the classroom. We would recommend that sessions be fifty minutes long and that they be scheduled for the last period in the morning or afternoon.

4. Keep the lines of communication open with the teachers. This may mean explaining to them the purpose of creative drama, the stages it tends to go through, and the effects it may have on the students' classwork. For example, if the students are missing important classwork, arrangements will have to be made whereby they can catch up without burdening the teachers with extra work after school.

Chapter 10

SERIAL STORY WRITING:
A THERAPEUTIC APPROACH WITH A
PHYSICALLY ABUSED ADOLESCENT

ONE SEPTEMBER, WHEN I was counseling in an elementary school, a seventh-grade teacher approached me with two stories written by a student in his English class. There was enough evidence in the stories to make the teacher concerned about whether the boy was "potentially dangerous and should be referred to a psychiatrist."

In the classroom, Tim was an isolate: he had few friends and got into fights easily. He was taller and bigger than the other boys. Although in the above-average range of intelligence, he was resistant to learning and had failed seventh grade the previous year. He was now repeating the grade with a new teacher.

The teacher thought Tim's learning problem was due to emotional factors rather than to any innate learning disability. He observed that Tim's performance was quite erratic and that persistent daydreaming and fantasy seemed to result in withdrawal, inattention, and off-task behaviors in the classroom.

In Tim's family he was the middle of three boys, all close together in age. His parents had recently separated. The boys lived with their mother and visited with their father on weekends. Tim had experienced considerable physical abuse.

Rationale for Treatment

The teacher was worried about Tim's explosive behavior in the classroom and the violent content of his fantasies. He was concerned that at a later date Tim might "kill someone."

I observed Tim in the classroom, read the stories, and felt there was justification for concern. However, I noticed that Tim was communicating his fantasies to his teacher by writing them down and handing them in as part of a class assignment. The thematic content of the stories revealed some positive ego strength and resourcefulness on Tim's part (see *Results* section below), and I felt that this material could form the basis of treatment.

The basis for this approach, as for art and drama therapy, is Jung's idea (1966) that in times of stress one can look to the patient's unconscious for understanding and direction. Jung believed that the healing potential of the psyche becomes activated when the client begins to symbolize fantasy material over a period of months. By this he means that psychological or inner growth occurs when dreams or daydreams are made tangible through some form of creative expression, such as writing or painting. He emphasized the importance of the "serial" approach whereby the counselor looks not at one dream or story but dreams or stories "in series, produced over time."

In the distressed person, the content of the dream or fantasy often reflects the "stuck" or blocked position and the origin of the disorder. If the client shares these images with a counselor, paints or writes them, Jung argued, psychological growth and movement are re-established. He called this approach "dream or symbol amplification," while he referred to the growth aspect of the unconscious as the "individuation process" (Jung, 1953). A Jungian therapist, then, takes his cues and direction from the unconscious of the client.

In regard to the present situation, I believed Tim needed some help with his fantasies and that the teacher needed some support and psychological insight in order to understand the boy's inner struggle.

Method

It was decided that Tim could write whatever he wanted during creative writing and that the teacher would bring the stories to me for discussion of their underlying psychological content. Tim was unaware of this consultation process, and my focus was on the teacher.

My approach to interpretation followed Jung's framework and raised hypotheses such as these: (a) every part of the story reflects a slightly different aspect of the writer's inner emotional life; (b) the emotions reach consciousness through the symbols used (i.e., the symbol is a container for a particular type of feeling); and (c) the mechanisms of repression and projection are frequently seen.

Results

From September to May, sixteen stories were collected. This averages approximately one story every two weeks. I chose nine stories for presentation here, which apparently depict the psychological struggle of the early adolescent to separate from his mother, father and brother and to function independently of them.

Included here with the stories are the notes and brief interpretations I discussed with the teacher.

1. THE DREAM

"You-who" said Aunt Pauli in a high-pitched voice. Quickly without listening to any more, I ran to Hell's Island. Step-after-step, gasp-after-gasp, I got away from the old nag. There was only one thing I didn't know. The Island was haunted and I was lost.

Trying to find my way home, I saw this dark and creepy figure. Without knowing what it was, it grabbed me, pulling me off the edge of the Island. All of a sudden, I remembered, from reading this book, a way to break this spell. I shouted, "Tag-along" and she disappeared.

Without thinking what to do, I went down to the ledge. Quickly I tied a rope to the stone and climbed my way up to the top. All of a sudden I woke up and found it was a relief to be in a dream.

The story seems to represent an attempt to escape from the critical ("You-who"), blaming aspects of the mother as symbolized by "Aunt Pauli," the "old nag." The problem is that where he runs to is no better. That is, one cannot run away from (i.e., repress) the feelings of anger at Mother because they will return to haunt one (in the form of a "dark and creepy figure"). Psychologically speaking, the feelings leave when they are looked at and integrated into conscious understanding.

Tim shows some resourcefulness in extricating himself from the grip of the unconscious and adapting ("I tied a rope to the stone and climbed my way up").

2. THE PHANTOM

It was Saturday, August 7, when we were robbed. My Mom's best jewelry was taken. John screamed, "Help!" I quickly ran to his room and he was dead. Gasping, I looked up and saw the phantom. He quickly took a swing at me with his razor-sharp axe. I ducked and grabbed him by his balls and landed right where it counts. I grabbed his axe and swung wildly at him. He gasped as I took both of his legs. I quickly dropped the axe and ran to the phone. I shouted frantically: "Operator, Operator, get me the police." All of a sudden his hand grabbed me and I fell to the floor in shock. It was the phantom. I ran out the door and saw the cops standing there and I told them he was in the house. They quickly phoned an ambulance and picked me up.

This is a classical oedipal theme in that it deals with the envy and jealousy at sharing Mother. He feels his father ("phantom") and probably his brother ("John") have more affection (i.e., "My Mom's best jewelry") than he does ("robbed"). This results in his need to render them "dead" and "castrated" ("I . . . grabbed him by his balls and landed right where it counts"), annihilating them so that he has Mother's undivided attention to himself. Naturally, this does not work because there is always an unconscious threat of retaliation by the ever-present, phantom father. In addition, taking Mom's best jewelry could express his repressed anger at her.

His inner strength and positive super-ego are once more evidenced by his coping ability and by the presence of the "cops" who phone for "an ambulance" (a helpful symbol).

I met with the teacher and father, encouraging them to spend a little time alone with Tim when they would be open to hearing his point of view and meeting some of his needs for attention. The teacher was already doing this, but it was difficult for the father to grasp the necessity of doing so. He usually made a request of Tim, rather than letting Tim tell him what he wanted to do with Dad or Mom. Over time, however, the father did begin to understand how important this was and did slowly change.

3. MY LAST NIGHT ALIVE

It was a cold, mysterious night when I noticed my Mom wasn't home. I called all her friends on the phone and found out that she wasn't there. Then I heard a shot coming from the direction of the backyard. She was lying there in agony, screaming for help. I called an ambulance but it was too late, she was dead. After five days I got over it and told my Dad. As the weeks went by, the sniper came back but what he didn't know was, I was ready for him. When I saw him climb on our roof, I got the sights right on him. The next morning I found out that the man was just repairing the roof. After explaining to the police, they took my gun and gave me a fine of $200. I raised the money in a week by helping my Mom's friends clean up the house. That night he came and shot me in the head, I died the same way my Mom did, in agony. I came down from the heavens and watched the murder. That night I was going to kill him. With all my spirit powers I drove him to his death.

This story reflects the ambivalence of the early adolescent—the wish to separate from the mother, to live independently of her, and the fear of doing just that. The separation is often manifested by tremendous rage and hurtful impulses, hence the emphasis on "shooting" and "agony." In other words, the separation only becomes possible when one has symbolically rendered the mother (or father) "dead." At this point one is psychologically free. But with the freedom comes the experience of pain, loneliness and loss (i.e., the desolation of the loss of dependency). In this case, Tim's separation is very brief, because he in turn is shot "in the head" (i.e., the center of consciousness) and returns once more into a state of unconsciousness and union with Mother ("I died the same way as my Mom").

This pattern is common. Psychic energy moves in a spiral fashion (Jung, 1960); that is, there is growth, then regression (i.e., a falling back into the unconscious), then more growth, regression, etc., until a new plane of psychic life is attained.

There is an ironic twist in the story: he mistakes the repairman for the sniper; that is, he "shoots" (or denies) someone who is trying to be helpful (probably his father). In reality, then, he is probably denying or refusing to see the helpful overtures that his father is making to him.

This denial is normal in adolescence, because—paradoxically—to respond to the parents' help results in remaining dependent on them. It is the normal experience of the "double bind." Growth comes from giving consciousness to both feelings, to struggling with the tension of opposites until there is a transformation and resolution. This does not occur here because the "death wish" (i.e. the sniper) wins out in the end, as the storyteller is "shot."

4. THE MAD DOG

Once in a lost village of Gorden there was a Dog. Everyone was afraid of it and when they saw it they would lock their doors and stay in.

That night, the Dog struck out. He ripped open the doors and murdered the people. In the morning there was a hunt for him. They broke up into groups: one took the lost lagoon and the other took the land. Searching quietly, one of the boys spotted him. The Dog came chasing him and killed our last man. Quickly I ran to the village and told the women to arm themselves with stakes. One-by-one, two-by-two, the women came out of their houses and the chase was on. I spotted him and speared him with the stake but he didn't die. Then I remembered how to kill him. I quickly got some salt and followed his trail of blood. I poured the salt down his mouth and he fell to the ground. Quickly it grabbed my legs and I fell to the ground in pain. All of a sudden it screamed. It was his last scream because he was dead and my people were safe.

Some emotional growth is demonstrated in this story, which reflects the heroic struggle between Tim's conscious ego and his murderous, aggressive instincts as represented by the Dog. Indeed, it is the classical tale of the youthful hero. The "last man" of the village is killed, and the boy-hero organizes the women in the chase. However, it is not brute strength that defeats the Dog, but knowledge and understanding.

Pouring salt down the mouth seems to be a symbolic attempt to reduce the pleasure that one experiences in dependency—much as antebuse is used in treating alcoholics. For psychological growth to occur, one has to transcend or sublimate one's oral needs. Here the oral-aggressive instincts are being doused or salted!

His relationship to the feminine is more positive in this story. Women are seen in a helpful role. This is important, because if the male denies the feminine principle he cuts himself off from any depth of love and leaves the psyche devoid of renewal and ongoing nourishment.

5. THE UNWELCOMED MAN

Three nights, three days, I had been waiting for the prize from the Daily Bugle, Rod and Reel Club. "Knock-knock. This is the Rod and Reel Club." Then all of a sudden the man pulled out a gun. My first reaction was to jump but then I realized that if I panicked he might shoot me. So I said: "What are you going to do with me?" All he did was laugh. Then as he fell asleep, I went into the kitchen and I pulled out twenty-five knives, three forks and two beef cutters. I rigged it so when he moved he would be filled with holes. I made a whole bunch of noise and he woke up. He pulled out his gun: "Ahh" he screamed. And there was silence; he was dead. But I got grounded for a month by my parents so see you next month.

This is another tale depicting the emerging young hero "waiting for the prize" and ending with killing the father. Often the adolescent male gets inflated (overkills) and has to be brought down to earth by the limits set by parents and teachers ("I got grounded for a month"). One sees here the typical adolescent intensity of negative affect toward father figures ("I pulled out twenty-five knives, three forks and two beef cutters"), and also a subliminal awareness that "winning the prize" (freedom and independence) is not going to be easy: you lose it just when you think you have it. For example, when he asks the man what he is going to do with him, the man just laughs as if to say: "So you thought you were going to win a prize!"

The story also reflects Tim's growing ego strength—that is, the growing mastery over his impulses by his intellect: "My first reaction was to jump but then I realized . . . he might shoot me." In other words, if he just reacts he will get into trouble. What he did was to use his head and ask a question.

Another variable here—and a sign of strength—is humor. Having been "grounded for a month," he closes by saying to the reader: "See you next month."

6. A PARCEL

It was Saturday when we saw this guy bring these giant boxes. After he left we looked and saw these boxes full of machine guns. We notified the police, and they set out a search for this man. Our description of him was exactly right but the guy said he didn't know a thing about it.

When we went home we read on one of the guns the name: Mr. Marcida. We dropped these parcels off and found out this guy worked for the Mafia. The next day we sent the police there and they asked for details. All the guy said was that he had a right to remain silent and all that jive. We followed him as he went to one of his gang meetings and we did a little snooping around. This guy asked us if we belonged here and we said, "Yes." Then he asked us if we knew the code. Luckily we heard another guy talking and saying the code. As we left we sent the whole cop squad to bring in the Mafia. We turned on the TV and saw that they had been brought in and the one who gave details would be rewarded $1,000.

This hero story reflects less violence and better-established controls. This time, Tim is no longer operating in isolation but is joined by his peers ("we"). In reality, he was beginning to make some friends in his class at this time.

His aggressive energy seemed more contained ("these giant boxes. . . . full of machine guns"), and there were no more gruesome details. One can see an ethical sense developing (and a super-ego) as he reports his findings to the police. This is a positive movement, as he abides by the rule of law and does not try to deal with the Mafia himself. On a subconscious level it might reflect a dawning awareness that, if he does not control his own violent feelings (the Mafia), he will end up like them—in trouble and in jail.

Once again, his resourcefulness is manifested throughout the story ("our description of him was exactly right. . . . we knew the code"), and this time it looks as if he will receive his reward!

7. HURRICANE

The wind was blowing and a hurricane was started. Powerful gusts of wind were hitting our area. Our family took cover. We packed boards against the windows and took cover behind strong support. Swish, a gust of wind took off the roof. Scared, I ran for more support: boards, tables, chairs and anything in my reach. "Ahh." My brother had been crushed by a board. I dashed to see if he was still alive. He was, but barely. I ran to get the first-aid kit but it was too late. He was dead. When I woke up, I found it was a bad dream.

Though Tim has been trying to contain his destructive impulses, this story reflects that the energy is still alive, strong enough to blow off the roof (i.e., to dismantle the controls) and to make him act out symbolically his death wish for his brother. His ambivalence is also reflected here as he tries to make good the injury with the first-aid kit.

Through these stories, Tim has expressed symbolically some of his unconscious feelings toward his mother, father, and brother. The next story seems to reflect his struggle more with the collective, archetypal forces of the unconscious (Jung, 1959) than with those of his personal unconscious.

8. THE THING

Half man, half monster, the incredible Thing noiselessly springs over towns. All is quiet until suddenly the stillness is shattered by a noise. The town spread wildly in excitement as the Thing struck. His green face and the strong, big arms were thrashing down, killing people. His strength was unreal. As seconds went by, changes came over his body. Armies surrounded the Thing and then in a split second rockets fired. Their purpose was to destroy the Thing. A spray came out of the rockets. The spray solidified into rock-hard ice covering the Thing. The Thing was now isolated from the world, but not for long. With all of his strength he tried to break the ice but could not. However, the heat from his body slowly melted the ice and freed him. From anger he became wild, swinging everywhere and trying to escape from the world. Then the army realized there was no other way but to kill him. Stung from the ice the Thing went for an attack. Using thick slabs of rock from the ground, he charged with fear.

The imagery Tim uses here, the movie-monster Thing, captures the crescendo of feeling. He gives voice to all of his rage—the rage that is impersonal and wants to destroy the whole world. The Thing reflects an archetypal energy source—the destructive force itself, originating in a very deep level of the psyche. The personal consciousness of the adolescent alone cannot contain this force. It needs the collective support of society. In earlier stories, support came from the police, in this one from the army. Tim attempts to use personal ingenuity to contain the Thing by the freezing process (i.e., by personal repression), but it does not hold for long.

In the adolescent phase of development, this destructive force can only be contained by the collective morality of society (Neumann, 1954). It is appropriate for Tim, then, that the "Thing" is eventually killed (i.e., repressed).

9. ESCAPE

For more than a mile the forest was left in blackened, bare desolation. I was lost in the darkest and coldest part of the forest. Walking at a steady pace I knew I would be out of this mess soon.

Then I heard a sharp scream. It was the scream of a hurt lady. I ran faster and faster until I reached the end of freedom. But I was trapped inside a cave and it wasn't a forest at all. Scitter, scatter, I heard slimy, dirty, ugly rats but then I knew there must be a way out. I would follow these rats until I was right on their tracks. This made them run faster and I knew it gave me a chance to get out. Then I saw light, the peek, a hole but only small enough for a rat to get through. Then, just within my reach, I touched something shiny with a slim, jagged edge. This would free me from this cave. I hammered and hammered until BANG I was free. I could now go home and tell my Mom the whole story.

The heroic struggle is over. Tim has fought his way through the pain, loneliness, and darkness of the unconscious and come through. In a psychological sense there is a rebirth—from being trapped inside the womb, to the struggle for freedom, to the scream of a "hurt lady." It seems that now he is free from infantile needs and, from the standpoint of a stronger self-concept, will be able to relate to his mother as a person in her own right. This means that his psychic energy and assertiveness can now be used for learning purposes and for relating to the outer world. By writing out these stories and sharing them with his teacher, he has worked his way through some of his inner-world conflicts and has emerged with a new identity, separate from the family.

During the year, Tim's explosive behavior diminished as did his frequent withdrawal into fantasy. He successfully completed seventh grade and was advanced to junior high, where eighteen months later he was maintaining good progress. Naturally, all this change was not due to serial story writing; that was but one aspect of a support system that involved input from his classroom teacher, other teachers in the school, and his family.

Discussion

Building a positive self-image or identity is a key developmental task of the adolescent (Erikson, 1968). Often this process involves considerable pain and anxiety as the child changes from boy to young man or girl to young woman. Historically, this difficult transition was facilitated by rituals we've termed the "rites of passage." Our culture no longer provides such protection, and our youth are frequently left to struggle on their own with this difficult phase of development (Tanner, 1970). Among recent efforts to address this vacuum is a manual by Allan and Dyck (1984) of contemporary transition activities for use by teachers, counselors and parents.

Jung (1964) notes that the adolescent's inner struggle parallels that described in hero myths. The search for one's own identity involves an initial separation from one's parents and often several difficult encounters with certain basic emotions and instincts —fear, rage, pain, loss, greed, envy, death, and re-birth. On the successful completion of the tasks, the hero returns home with a new identity, enabling him to relate to his parents more or less as equals without undue dependency.

This process is clearly depicted in these stories of Tim's, where one sees the act of separation ("without listening to any more, I ran to Hell's Island"), the continual struggle with basic impulses, the

pull between feelings of dependency and independence, the ac-
complishment of heroic tasks, and the emergence of a developing
conscience and super-ego. This is followed in the last story by a
psychological re-birth (i.e., the solidifying of a new identity) which
lets Tim conclude: "I could now go home and tell my Mom the
whole story."

Tim's stories give one a picture of the unconscious "at work." In
them, one can see the themes reflecting the slow maturation and
evolution of the storyteller's personality. For example, in the early
stories, the storyteller is struggling to survive, often overwhelmed
by destructive and aggressive impulses, while near the end of the
series he demonstrates mastery and effective coping in the face of
threat.

On a more general level, serial story writing can be a helpful approach for teachers and counselors to use with children who
display excessive fantasy behavior. When fantasy material is symbolized in some form of creative expression, given definite
time–space boundaries (i.e., in Tim's case, in a creative writing
class and in a special notebook), and tied to a caring relationship
(his teacher), psychological growth can occur (Allan, 1977,
1978a; and Wallace, 1973). When these conditions are not met,
fantasy behavior becomes time-consuming, circular in nature (i.e.,
the same fantasies erupt time and time again with no psychological
growth or change in content) and disruptive to learning (Klein,
1976).

Chapter 11

SANDPLAY

SAND OFTEN ACTS as a magnet for children. Before they realize it their hands are sifting, making tunnels, shaping mountains, runways and riverbeds. When miniature toys are added, a whole world appears, dramas unfold and absorption is total.

Background

According to Stewart (1982), the first description of sandplay as a counseling technique came from the British pediatrician Margaret Lowenfeld (1939). In the 1930s, she established the London Institute of Child Psychology. She recalls reading H. G. Well's (1911) book *Floor Games* where he describes the great animation he felt when he and his two boys played on the floor with miniature soldiers.

In her institute, Lowenfeld added two zinc trays to the playroom, one half filled with sand and the other with some water and implements for shaping. The toys were placed in a box, and the children who came to the institute combined the toys with the sandplay and started to call this box of toys "the world." In turn, Lowenfeld (1979) called this method of play "The World Technique."

The method was brought to the United States by Buhler (1951) who used sandplay mainly for diagnosis and research. However, it is the Swiss Jungian analyst Dora Kalff (1966, 1981) who has had the greatest impact on developing the approach, formulating theoretical principles and training many practitioners throughout the world.

Expanding on the works of Neumann (1954, 1973), Kalff sees the development of a healthy ego as a critically important task for

212

children. The function of the ego is to balance and mediate between inner drives and the outer world. To Kalff, the ego is
strengthened by a deep internal feeling of mother–child unity
which develops slowly from birth and which culminates during the
second and third years of life. Disturbed children are those who
have experienced breaks in bonding which damage the inner feeling of wholeness and impair ego functioning. In sandplay, the
child has the opportunity to resolve the traumas through externalizing the fantasies and by developing a sense of a relationship
and control over inner impulses through play. It is the connection
to unconscious drives, especially the archetype of the Self, and
their expression in symbolic form that greatly facilitate healthy
psychological functioning.

Method

The sandtray itself is a container approximately 20-x-30-x-3 in-
ches. Usually two are made available. They are waterproofed: one
to contain dry sand and the other damp. The inside is painted blue
to simulate water when the sand is pushed to the side. The dimensions are important and specific, so that the sandworld can be
taken in at a glance without unnecessary head movement. As well,
hundreds of miniature toys and objects from which the child may
choose are made available. Categories include:

> People: domestic, military, fantasy, mythological
> Buildings: houses, schools, churches, castles
> Animals: tame, wild, zoo, prehistoric, marine
> Vehicles: land, air, water, space, war machines
> Vegetation: trees, shrubs, plants, vegetables
> Structures: bridges, fences, gates, doorways, corrals
> Natural objects: shells, driftwood, stones, bones, eggs
> Symbolic objects: wishing wells, treasure chests, jewelry

Some counselors place the toys in categories on shelves so they
are readily visible (fig. 11.1). Others present them randomly on a

213

FIG. 11.1   Toys on shelves

large table. It is recommended that "families" of items be available, such as a sow and a litter, three dinosaurs, four snakes and a small doll family.

Sandplay is the process, sandtray the medium, and sandworld the finished product. The process begins when the counselor invites the child to play with the sand and to choose from the assortment of miniatures. Each object, with its own physical structure and symbolic meaning, triggers a fantasy reaction. Kalff (1981) believes that "the symbols speak for inner, energy laden pictures of the innate potentials of the human being" (p. 29) which, when expressed, facilitate emotional growth.

The counselor plays a key role in providing the "safe and protected space" where the inner drama and healing potential of the psyche can unfold. This "safe and protected space" is the sandtray and the therapeutic relationship. Most practitioners emphasize the value of unconditional positive regard and minimal verbalizations by the counselor. Interpretation is seldom needed because the psychological issues are resolved or understood on an uncon-scious, symbolic level. The counselor is there as a witness to the process of play, which makes the inner problem visible and allows for therapeutic movement and growth. Toward the end of a ses-sion a child may announce "goodbye," "I'm finished" or just sit silently in front of the sandworld. Often, then, there is a point where the process of play stops and a finished work is evidenced.

Buhler (1951) developed an observation form on which one may record prevalent themes in the play, and Reed (1975) devised a rating scale for children. Some counselors draw a quick sketch, while most take a slide photograph of each sandworld. At the ter-mination of treatment (usually after eight to ten sessions in the schools), the counselor shows the child all the slides as a means of review and discussion.

Overview of Common Stages in Sandplay

As the sand drama and play unfold, children tend to portray chaos, struggle (organized fighting) and resolution in recurring cycles.

Chaos. In this stage, often the first, the child may literally "dump" ten to three hundred toys and objects into the sandtray. There is no order—just a vast upheaval and intermingling of sand and toys. The toys do not seem to be chosen deliberately. There may be an absence of animal, plant or human life. The land may be barren and dry, and often crops or vegetation are in ruins. This stage reflects and objectifies the emotional turmoil and chaos in the child's life. In other words, the child's ego may be over-whelmed by distressing emotions. Depictions of this stage may oc-cur once or continue for two to three counseling sessions or even longer.

Struggle. Many battles occur as monsters fight monsters, robot man wipes out armies and knights tirelessly joust each other. Anything that moves is shot, destroyed or blown up. Often, in the beginning, both sides are annihilated; there is no winner and the dead are left in a heap in the corner. Over the weeks, the battles become more intense, more organized, and the struggles more balanced. The adversaries are not killed but imprisoned, and a hero emerges who wins in the battle against the "dark forces" (i.e., destructive impulses).

Resolution. In this phase, life seems to be getting "back to normal." Order is being restored, and there is a balance between nature, people and the rhythm of daily life. Animals are in their correct habitat; fences protect the sheep and cattle. Roadways wind evenly through town and country, and the crops and trees bear fruit. The counselor senses a resolution of a problem and the feeling that the child is accepting his or her place in the outer world. Often the child will say, "I don't need to come any more," and this is usually confirmed by the teacher. Symbolically, the feeling of completion and wholeness is apparent in images of squares, rectangles and circles (Kalff, 1981; Kellogg, 1970). There is an ordering of the sandworld and an integration of libidinal forces manifested earlier.

Teachers' Reactions to Sandplay

When children return to the classroom after sandplay, teachers frequently comment on their calmer, relaxed mood, their ability to become involved in their work, and the presence of a sense of humor. After eight to ten sessions, there is often dramatic improvement and the child begins to respond to normal teacher controls and limit-setting.

Noyes (1981) found that, when sandplay was used as part of her remedial reading program for sixth graders, it deepened rapport and intimacy, improved self-esteem, helped resolve inner conflicts and increased reading scores in all students from a range of two to five and a half years.

Case Study

James (a pseudonym), a second grader, was referred for counseling because he exhibited inappropriate behavior in the classroom and on the playground. Two years earlier, he was moved several hundred miles to live with his father, whom he did not know, his step-mother and her two older girls. When introduced to sandplay, he immediately became involved with the materials.

Session 1. Many animals and vehicles (cars, trucks, jet planes) were precariously and chaotically piled at one end of the sandtray, held down by two snakes. At the bottom of the pile was Pegasus, the winged horse, and a jet. It appeared that Pegasus and the jet, despite all their power, were unable to move out from under this serpent domination and control (fig. 11.2).

Session 2. Many of the same objects were used, but this time there was order and regulation. The planes and the police

FIG. 11.2   Chaos: Pegasus trapped

217

helicopter were ready for take-off. The cars and trucks were lined up as if waiting for a signal to go. One ambulance was in readiness in the corner. All of the animals, however, were prone. It was as if they could not move even though they were no longer in the grip of the snakes. The exceptions were a crocodile, a snake and a tiger sliding toward each other across a lake as if in preparation for attack and a fight (fig. 11.3).

Sessions 3, 4 and 5. These sandtrays showed more organization. Vehicles were stationed in appropriate bays. There were a house, a boy and two women. A tree grew in one corner and Pegasus reappeared. Just before he left session five, James placed two men in the sandtray: an older man with the two women and a younger man by himself in the corner (fig. 11.4).

Sessions 6 and 7. There followed two sandworlds whose themes appeared to be extensions of the other sessions but yet more enriched. Animals were standing. There was more growth, symbolized by trees and foliage, and a red wizard, a magical helper, was riding Pegasus.

Sessions 8 and 9. The theme and toys were similar, but to this world James added several black wizard helpers. As he was leaving to go back to the classroom, he returned to the sandtray and silently added Pegasus. Then he stood the younger man on his feet. He turned and left the counseling room.

During this period, in counseling, James painted two pictures: the first showed a fox hiding from a mammoth creature. The fox had several places to hide. The second depicted two mammoth creatures in the water with a small fish swimming between. He added a castle and a Canadian flag. In the castle, the king stood watch.

Session 10. This was his last sandworld. In it James showed a circle of his family members, including the older man. The family truck and a house were in evidence as was a jet plane—all part of the circle (fig. 11.5). After a period of concentrated attention, James placed Pegasus in the center of the family circle. James looked up and smiled as he quietly said, "He's magic, you know, and no one can see him but the boy."

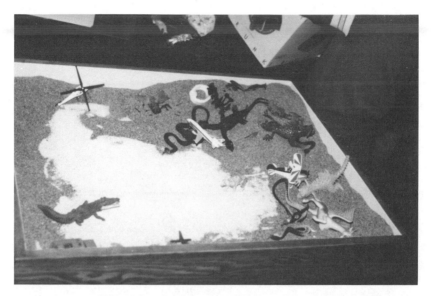

FIG. 11.3   Struggle: Crocodile vs. snake and tiger

FIG. 11.4   Resolution: Organization

FIG. 11.5   Resolution: Pegasus freed

Discussion

At first, during counseling, James was quiet and tentative. He tended to ignore the counselor and immersed himself totally in his worlds and paintings. Slowly he came out of himself and began to talk more about his sandworlds and his dreams.

In the sandtrays one sees the movement from chaos to struggle to resolution. The early phase of chaos reflects the inner turmoil in James: many of his emotions are confused and intertwined. He cannot use the energy of the jet (a symbol of adaptive movement in the outer world) and the energy of Pegasus (a symbol of inner strength) to help him in his life. He is feeling controlled and trapped by negative external forces (as symbolized by the snakes). His ego is overwhelmed by psychological pain (Allan, 1978). In the subsequent session one sees the slow process of differentiation, regulation, and separation of various emotions, as symbolized by planes, trucks and an ambulance. The animals are not active (i.e., they are prone) except for three aggressive forces (crocodile, snake and tiger). Slowly, family members appear, as do "helpers" and symbols of vegetative and instinctual life. Order and identity are restored (the king and the Canadian flag), and the family appears more intact. It is interesting to note the key role Pegasus plays throughout. Commonly, children will be attracted to one significant symbol that will appear, disappear and reappear throughout their treatment (Allan, 1986). Pegasus, of course, is invisible. He reflects the healthy essence of the boy's spirit which has now become alive again in him.

Treatment ended when the school term did. Follow-up indicated that his impulsive, aggressive behavior diminished, his social skills improved and he was channeling his energy into art and soccer.

Conclusions

Sandplay as a technique for counseling elementary children may be implemented by counselors who have had basic training in play therapy. Kalff (1981) warns against the use of interpretation. The crux of sandplay therapy is not that it must be interpreted but that it must be witnessed respectfully. The counselor's attitude for this process is "active being" rather than direction and guidance. The process of play and dramatization seems to release blocked psychic energy and to activate the self-healing potential that Jung (1964) believed is embedded in the human psyche.

Sandplay counseling is challenging and knows no age barriers. It has been used with children as young as two years old and with adults of all ages. The unleashing of repressed energy transforms that energy so that it may work productively for personality development and for future learning.

Appendix A

THE ROSEBUSH: A GUIDED FANTASY

I WOULD LIKE you to close your eyes. Just be aware of your body. Forget about what's been going on around you . . . just think about what's going on inside of you. Think about your breathing . . . feel the air move in through your nose and mouth, down into your chest—imagine that your breathing is like gentle waves lapping on the shore. . . . As each wave rolls in, the more relaxed you feel.

Think about your right arm. Feel it getting heavier and heavier. . . . Feel the heaviness go all the way down the arm, down to your fingertips. . . . Think about your left arm. . . . Feel it getting heavier and heavier. . . . Feel the heaviness go all the way down the arm, down to your fingertips. . . . Think about your right leg. . . . Feel it getting heavier and heavier. . . . Feel the heaviness go down, down, into your foot. . . . Think about your left leg. . . . Feel it getting heavier and heavier. . . . Feel the heaviness go down, down, into your foot. . . . Feel your body relaxing and feeling heavy. . . .

Be aware of your thoughts and images in your mind . . . look at them [pause] . . . now put them into a glass jar and watch them . . . [pause] examine them. As more thoughts and images come into your mind, put them into your jar too. . . . Find out what you can learn about them. . . . Now take the jar and pour out the thoughts and images, watch as they spill out and disappear [pause] . . . the jar is empty. . . .

Now I'd like you to imagine that you are a rosebush. Become a rosebush and find out what it's like to be a rosebush. . . . What kind of rosebush are you? . . . Are you very small? . . . Are you large? . . . Are you wide? . . . Are you tall? . . . Do you have flowers? . . . If so, what kind? . . . They can be any kind you want. . . . Do you have leaves? . . . What kind? . . . What are your stems and branches like? . . . Do you have thorns? . . . What are your roots like [pause] . . . or maybe you don't have any. . . . If you do, are they long and straight? . . . Are they twisted? . . . Are they deep? . . . Look around you [pause] . . . are you in a yard? . . . in a park? . . . in the desert? . . . in the city? . . . in the country? . . . in the middle of the ocean? . . . Are you in a pot or growing in the ground . . .

or through cement . . . or even inside somewhere? . . . Look around you [pause] . . . what do you see? . . . Other flowers? . . . Are you alone? . . . Are there any trees? . . . Animals? . . . People? . . . Birds? . . . Do you look like a rosebush or something else? . . . Is there anything around you like a fence? . . . Does someone take care of you? . . . What's the weather like for you right now?

What is your life like? . . . How do you feel? . . . What do you experience and what happens to you as the seasons change? . . . Be aware of yourself as a rosebush . . . look carefully. Find out how you feel about your life and what happens to you.

In a few minutes, I'll ask you to open your eyes and I want you to draw a picture of yourself as a rosebush. Then, later I'll ask you a few questions, and I'll want you to tell me about the picture as though you are the rosebush [longer pause]. . . . When you are ready, open your eyes and draw the rosebush.

Appendix B

POST-DRAWING INQUIRY FOR THE ROSEBUSH

Question One:	What kind of rosebush are you, and what do you look like?
Question Two:	Tell me about your flowers.
Question Three:	Tell me about your leaves.
Question Four:	Tell me about your stems and branches.
Question Five:	Do you have thorns? If so, tell me about them. If not, tell me how you protect yourself. Are you a mean or a friendly rosebush?
Question Six:	Tell me about your roots.
Question Seven:	Tell me about where you live. What kind of things do you see around you? How do you like living where you are?
Question Eight:	Do you think that you look like a rosebush, or do you think that you look like something else? If so, what?
Question Nine:	Who takes care of you? How do you feel about that? How do they look after you?
Question Ten:	What's the weather like for you right now? What happens to you as the seasons change?
Question Eleven:	How does it feel to be a rosebush? What is your life like as a rosebush?

References

Chapter 1

Allan, J. A. B. (1975). A baby clinic in an elementary school: Towards an integration of family, school and community life. *Canadian Counsellor* 9: 102-11.

Allan, J., and Nairne, N. (1984). *Class discussions in the elementary school for teachers and counselors.* Toronto: Univ. of Toronto Guidance Center Press.

Axline, V. (1947). *Play therapy.* Boston: Houghton Mifflin.

Bakan, P. (1976). The right brain is the dreamer. *Psychology Today* 10: 66-68.

Baruch, D. W. (1949). *New ways in discipline.* New York: McGraw-Hill.

Fordham, M. (1957). *New developments in analytical psychology.* London: Routledge and Kegan Paul.

Ginott, H. (1972). *Teacher and child.* New York: Macmillan.

Gordon, T. (1970). *Parent effectiveness training.* New York: Wyden.

Jung, C. G. (1956). *The collected works.* Vol. 5, *Symbols of transformation.* Princeton: Princeton Univ. Press.

_____. (1964). *Man and his symbols.* Garden City, N.Y.: Doubleday.

Neumann, E. (1954). *The origins and history of consciousness.* Princeton: Princeton Univ. Press.

Ornstein, R. (1972). *Psychology of consciousness.* San Francisco: Freeman.

Rossi, E. (1977). The cerebral hemispheres in analytical psychology. *Journal of Analytical Psychology* 22: 32-51.

Chapter 2

Allan, J. (1977). The use of creative drama with acting-out sixth and seventh grade boys and girls. *Canadian Counsellor* 11: 135-43.

_____. (1978a). Serial drawing: A therapeutic approach with young children. *Canadian Counsellor* 12: 223-28.

_____. (1978b). Serial story writing: A therapeutic approach with a physically abused young adolescent. *Canadian Counsellor* 12: 132-37.

_____. (1978c). Facilitating emotional and symbolic communication in young children. *Journal of Canadian Association for Young Children* 4: 8-19.

_____. (1986). The body in child psychotherapy. In *The body in analysis*, ed. N. Schwartz-Salant and M. Stein, 145–66. Wilmette, IL.: Chiron Publications.

Allan, J., and Barber, J. (1986). Teacher needs and counselor response: One example. *Elementary School Guidance and Counseling* 20: 277–82.

Allan, J., and Berry, P. (1987). Sandplay. *Elementary School Guidance and Counseling* 21: 300–06.

Allan, J., and Clark, M. (1985). Art counselling in elementary schools and child guidance clinics. *Canadian Journal of Art Therapy* 2: 23–31.

Allan, J.; Doi, K.; and Reed, C. (1979). Need assessment: A survey of B.C.'s principals, primary and intermediate teachers' perception of counselling needs. *Canadian Counsellor* 14: 132–37.

Allan, J., and MacDonald, R. (1975). The use of fantasy enactment in the treatment of an emerging autistic child. *Journal of Analytical Psychology* 20: 57–68.

Buck, J. (1948). The H-T-P test. *Journal of Clinical Psychology* 4: 151–59.

Buttery, J., and Allan, J. (1981). Journal writing as a developmental guidance method. *Canadian Counsellor* 15: 134–38.

Carkhuff, R. (1969). *Helping and human relationships*, vol. 1. New York: Holt, Rinehart & Winston, Inc.

Jung, C. G. (1959). *The collected works*. Vol. 9, i, *The archetypes and the collective unconscious*. Princeton: Princeton Univ. Press.

_____. (1965). *Memories, dreams, reflections*. New York: Random House.

_____. (1966). *The collected works*. Vol. 16, *The practice of psychotherapy*. Princeton: Princeton Univ. Press.

Neumann, E. (1974). *The great mother*. Princeton: Princeton Univ. Press.

Schwartz-Salant, N. (1986). On the subtle-body concept in clinical practice. In *The body in analysis*, ed. N. Schwartz-Salant and M. Stein, 19–58. Wilmette, IL.: Chiron Publications.

Thompson, F., and Allan, J. (1985). Art counselling in the elementary schools: A method of active intervention. *Guidance and Counselling* 1 (2): 63–73.

Chapter 3

Silver, R. A. (1978). *Developing cognitive and creative skills through art.* Baltimore: University Park Press.

Stewart, L. H. (1987). Affect and archetype in analysis. In *Archetypal processes in psychotherapy*, ed. N. Schwartz-Salant and M. Stein, 131–62. Wilmette, IL.: Chiron Publications.

Chapter 4

Allan, J. (1978). Serial drawing: A therapeutic approach with young children. *Canadian Counsellor* 12: 223-28.

Allan, J., and Clark, M. (1984). Directed art counselling. *Elementary School Guidance and Counseling* 19: 116-24.

Anderson, R. (1980). Using guided fantasy with children. *Elementary School Guidance and Counseling* 14: 39-46.

Bellak, L. (1954). A study of limitations and "failures": Toward an ego psychology of projective techniques. *Journal of Projective Techniques* 18: 279-93.

Bolander, K. (1977). *Assessing personality through tree drawings.* New York: Basic Books.

Borg, W., and Gall, M. (1983). *Educational research: An introductory text.* 4th ed. New York: Longman.

Elkisch, P. (1960). Free art expression. In *Projective techniques with children,* ed. A. I. Rabin and M. R. Haworth, 273-88. New York: Grune & Stratton.

Fino, J. (1978). Guided imagery and movement as a means to help disturbed children draw together. *American Journal of Art Therapy* 18: 3-9.

Gamna, G., and Bortino, R. (1980). Introduction to an evaluation of art therapy. *Confinia Psychiatria* 23: 15-25.

Harrower, M. (1954). Clinical aspects of failure in the projective techniques. *Journal of Projective Techniques* 18: 294-302.

Korner, A. (1956). Limitations of projective techniques: Apparent and real. *Journal of Projective Techniques* 20: 42-47.

Oaklander, V. (1978). *Windows to our children.* Moab, UT.: Real People Press.

Pinholster, R. (1983). From dark to light: The use of drawing to counsel nonverbal children. *Elementary School Guidance and Counseling* 17: 268-73.

Rabin, A. I., ed. (1981). *Assessment with projective techniques.* New York: Springer.

Roosa, L. (1981). Family drawing / storytelling technique: An approach to assessment of family dynamics. *Elementary School Guidance and Counseling* 15: 269-72.

Singer, J. (1981). Research applications of projective methods. In *Assessment with projective techniques,* ed. A. I. Rabin, 297-331. New York: Springer.

Stevens, J. (1971). *Awareness: Exploring, experimenting, experiencing.* Moab, UT.: Real People Press.

Wechsler, D. (1974). *Manual of the Wechsler Intelligence Scale for Children—Revised.* New York: Psychological Corporation.

References

Wittmer, J., and Myrick, R. (1980). *Facilitative teaching.* 2d ed. Minneapolis: Educational Media Corporation.

Chapter 5

Allan, J. (1978). Serial drawing: A therapeutic approach with young children. *Canadian Counsellor* 12: 223–28.

Allan, J., and Clark, M. (1984). Directed art counselling. *Elementary School Guidance and Counseling* 19: 116–24.

Allan, J., and Crandall, J. (1986). The rosebush: A visualization strategy for possible identification of child abuse. *Elementary School Guidance and Counseling* 21: 44–51.

Bach, S. R. (1966). Spontaneous painting of severely ill patients: A contribution to psychosomatic medicine. *Acta psychosomatica* 8: 1–66.

———. (1975). Spontaneous drawings of leukemic children as an expression of the total personality, mind and body. *Acta Paedopsychiatrica* 41 (3): 86–104.

Bertoia, J., and Allan, J. (1988). School management of the bereaved child. *Elementary School Guidance and Counseling* 23.

Bluebond-Langner, M. (1978). *The private worlds of dying children.* Princeton: Princeton Univ. Press.

Cooper, J. C. (1978). *An illustrated encyclopaedia of traditional symbols.* London: Thames & Hudson Ltd.

Furth, G. M. (1981). The use of drawings made at critical times in one's life. In *Living with death and dying,* ed. E. Kubler-Ross, 63–94. New York: Macmillan.

Kiepenheuer, K. (1980). Spontaneous drawings of a leukemic child: An aid for more comprehensive care of fatally ill children and their families. *Psychosomatische Medizin* 9: 21–32.

Kubler-Ross, E. (1983). *On children and death.* New York: Macmillan.

Storm, H. (1972). *Seven arrows.* New York: Harper & Row.

Thompson, F., and Allan, J. (1987). Common symbols of children in art counseling. *Guidance and Counselling* 2 (5): 24–32.

Williams, Y. B., and Furth, G. M. (1985). Getting to know ourselves. Privately published workshop manual, 4th ed.

Chapter 6

Bachelard, G. (1971). *On poetic imagination and reverie.* Trans. Colette Gaudin. Rev. ed. Dallas: Spring Publications.

———. (1983). *Water and dreams.* Trans. Edith R. Farrell. Dallas: The Dallas Institute Publications.

Champernowne, I. (1971). Art and therapy: An uneasy partnership. *American Journal of Art Therapy* 18: 131–43.

Chapman, L. (1982). *Instant art, instant culture: The unspoken policy for American schools.* New York: Teacher's College Press.

Churchill, A. (1971). *Art for pre-adolescents.* New York: McGraw-Hill.

Drachnik, C. (1976). A historical relationship between art therapy and art education and the possibilities for future integration. *Art Education* 29 (7): 16–24.

Kramer, E. (1975). The problem of quality in art. In *Art therapy in theory and practice,* ed. E. Ulman and P. Dachinger, 43–59. New York: Schocken Books.

Michael, J., ed. (1982). *The Lowenfeld lectures.* University Park: Pennsylvania State Univ. Press.

Pine, S. (1975). Fostering growth through art education, art therapy and in art in psychotherapy. In *Art therapy in theory and practice,* ed. E. Ulman and P. Dachinger, 60–94. New York: Schocken Books.

Robertson, S. M. (1982). *Rosegarden and labyrinth: A study in art education.* Dallas: Spring Publications.

Tritten, G. (1964). *Art techniques for children.* New York: Reinhold.

Chapter 7

Allan, J. (1978). Serial drawing: A therapeutic approach with young children. *Canadian Counsellor* 12: 223–28.

Allan, J., and Clark, M. (1984). Directed art counselling. *Elementary School Guidance and Counseling* 19: 116–24.

Alschuler, R. H., and Hattwick, L. A. (1943). Easel painting as an index of personality in pre-school children. *Journal of Orthopsychiatry* 13: 616–25.

———. (1969). *Painting and personality: A study of young children.* 2d ed. Chicago: Univ. of Chicago Press.

Bieber, I., and Herkimer, J. (1948). Art in psychotherapy. *American Journal of Psychiatry* 104: 627–37.

References

Birren, F. (1969). *Light, color, and environment.* New York: Van Nostrand Reinhold.

———. (1978). *Color, psychology and color psychotherapy.* Syracuse, N.Y.: Citadel Press.

Bluestein, V. (1978). Loss of a loved one and the drawing of dead and broken branches on the H-T-P. *Psychology in the Schools* 15: 56-59.

Brink, M. (1944). Mental hygiene value of children's artwork. *American Journal of Orthopsychology* 14: 136-46.

Buck, J. N. (1948). The H-T-P technique: A qualitative and quantitative scoring manual. *Journal of Clinical Psychology* 4: 319-96.

———. (1978). *The house-tree-person technique.* Rev. ed. Los Angeles: Western Psychological Services.

Burns, R. C., and Kaufman, S. H. (1970). *Kinetic family drawings.* New York: Brunner/Mazel.

Cooper, J. C. (1978). *An illustrated encyclopaedia of traditional symbols.* London: Thames & Hudson Ltd.

de Vries, A. (1976). *Dictionary of symbols and imagery.* London: North-Holland Press.

di Leo, J. H. (1970). *Young children and their drawings.* New York: Brunner/Mazel.

Jolles, I. (1957). Some advances in the interpretation of the chromatic phase of the H-T-P. *Journal of Clinical Psychology* 13: 81-89.

Jung, C. G. (1964). *Man and his symbols.* Garden City, N.Y.: Doubleday.

Kadis, A. (1950). Fingerpainting as a projective technique. In *Projective psychology,* ed. L. Abt and L. Ballak. New York: Knopf.

McNiff, S. (1986). *Educating the creative arts therapist.* Springfield, IL.: Charles C. Thomas.

———. (1988). *Fundamentals of art therapy.* Springfield, IL.: Charles C. Thomas.

Napoli, P. (1946). Fingerpainting and personality diagnosis. *Genetic Psychology Monograph* 34: 129-31.

Naumburg, M. (1966). *Dynamically oriented art therapy: Its principles and practice.* London: Grune & Stratton.

Pasto, T. (1968). The bio-mythology of color: A theory. In *Psychiatry and art,* ed. I. Jakab. Basel, Switzerland: South Kargar.

Precker, Z. A. (1950). Painting and drawing in personality assessment. *Journal of Projective Research* 14: 262-86.

Rubin, J. A. (1978). *Child art therapy.* New York: Van Nostrand Reinhold.

Spencer, V. (1969). The use of water colors to increase chromatic H-T-P productivity. In *Advances in the H–T–P techniques: Variations and applications,* ed. J. N. Buck and E. F. Hammer. Los Angeles: Western Psychological Services.

Thompson, F., and Allan, J. (1985). Art counselling in the elementary schools: A method of active intervention. *Guidance and Counselling* 1 (2): 63–73.

Zimmerman, J., and Garfunkel, L. (1942). Preliminary studies of the art production of adult psychotics. *Psychiatric Quarterly* 14: 313–18.

Chapter 8

Allan, J. A. B. (1976). The identification and treatment of "difficult babies." *Canadian Nurse* 72 (12): 11–16.

———. (1986). The body in child psychotherapy. In *The body in analysis,* ed. N. Schwartz-Salant and M. Stein, 145–66. Wilmette, IL.: Chiron Publications.

Anthony, J. (1958). An experimental approach to the psychotherapy of childhood: Autism. *British Journal of Medical Psychology* 31: 311–35.

Bergman, P., and Escalona, S. K. (1949). Unusual sensitiveness in very young children. *Psychoanalytic Study of the Child* 4: 333–452.

Bettelheim, B. (1967). *The empty fortress.* New York: The Free Press.

Fordham, K. (1966). Notes on the psychotherapy of infantile autism. *British Journal of Medical Psychology* 39: 299–312.

Klein, M. (1955). Psycho-analytic play technique: Its history and significance. *New Directions in Psycho-Analysis.* London: Tavistock.

Chapter 9

Allan, J., and MacDonald, R. (1975). The use of fantasy enactment in the treatment of an emerging autistic child. *Journal of Analytical Psychology* 20: 57–68.

Dinkmeyer, D., and Muro, J. (1971). *Group counseling: Theory and practice.* Itasca, IL.: Peacock.

Erikson, E. H. (1968). *Identity, youth and crisis.* New York: Norton.

Freud, A. (1948). *Ego and the mechanics of defense.* New York: International Univ. Press.

Hartup, W. W. (1970). Peer interaction and social organization. In *Carmichael's manual of child psychology,* ed. P. H. Mussen, vol. 1. 3rd ed. New York: Wiley.

References

Kohlberg, L. (1970). *Stages in the development of moral thought and action.* New York: Holt, Rinehart & Winston.

Kramer, R. (1968). Changes in moral judgement response pattern during late adolescence and young adulthood. Ph.D. diss., University of Chicago.

Layman, G. (1976). *Educational drama for six to twelve-year olds.* Toronto: Methuen.

Mildiner, L., and House, W. (1975). *The gates.* London: Centerprise Publishing Project.

Offer, D. (1969). *The psychological world of the teenager.* New York: Basic Books.

Piaget, J. (1948). *The moral judgement of the child.* New York: Free Press.

Spolin, V. (1963). *Improvisation for the theatre.* Chicago: Northwestern Univ. Press.

Sutton-Smith, B., and Savasta, M. (1972). Sex differences in play and power. Paper presented at annual meeting of Eastern Psychological Association, Boston.

Tanner, J. M. (1970). Physical growth. In *Carmichael's manual of child psychology,* ed. P. H. Mussen, vol. 1. 3rd ed. New York: Wiley.

Wallace, E. (1973). Conventional boundaries or protective temenos. *Art Psychotherapy* 1 (2): 91-99.

Way, B. (1967). *Development through drama.* London: Longman.

Chapter 10

Allan, J. (1977). The use of creative drama with acting-out sixth and seventh grade boys and girls. *Canadian Counsellor* 11: 135-43.

_____. (1978a). Facilitating emotional and symbolic communication in young children. *Journal of Canadian Association for Young Children* 4: 8-19.

_____. (1978b). Serial drawing: A therapeutic approach with young children. *Canadian Counsellor* 12: 223-28.

Allan, J. A. B., and Dyck, P. (1984). Transition: Childhood to adolescence. *Elementary School Guidance and Counseling* 19: 277-86.

Erikson, E. H. (1968). *Identity, youth and crisis.* New York: Norton.

Jung, C. G. (1953). *The collected works.* Vol. 7, *Two essays on analytical psychology.* Princeton: Princeton Univ. Press.

_____. (1959). *The collected works.* Vol. 9, i, *The archetypes and the collective unconscious.* Princeton: Princeton Univ. Press.

_____. (1960). *The collected works.* Vol. 8, *The structure and dynamics of the psyche.* Princeton: Princeton Univ. Press.

_____. (1964). *The collected works.* Vol. 17, *The development of personality.* Princeton: Princeton Univ. Press.

_____. (1966), *The collected works* Vol. 16, *The practice of psychotherapy.* Princeton: Princeton Univ. Press.

Klein, M. (1976). *The psychoanalysis of children.* New York: Dell.

Neumann, E. (1954). *The origins and history of consciousness.* Princeton: Princeton Univ. Press.

Tanner, J. M. (1970). Physical growth. In *Carmichael's manual of child psychology,* ed. P. H. Mussen, vol. 1. 3rd ed. New York: Wiley.

Wallace, E. (1973). Conventional boundaries or protective temenos. *Art Psychotherapy* 1 (2): 91-99.

Chapter 11

Allan, J. (1978). Serial drawing: A therapeutic approach with young children. *Canadian Counsellor* 12: 223-28.

_____. (1986). The body in child psychotherapy. In *The body in analysis,* ed. N. Schwartz-Salant and M. Stein, 145-66. Wilmette, IL.: Chiron Publications.

Buhler, C. (1951). The world test: A projective technique. *Journal of Child Psychiatry* 2: 4-23.

Jung, C. G. (1964). *Man and his symbols.* Garden City, N.Y.: Doubleday.

Kalff, D. M. (1966). *Sandspiel.* Zürich: Rascher Verlag.

_____. (1981). *Sandplay: A psychotherapeutic approach to the psyche.* Boston: Sigo Press.

Kellogg, R. (1970). *Analyzing children's art.* Palo Alto, CA.: Mayfield Publishing Company.

Lowenfeld, M. (1939). The world pictures of children. *British Journal of Medical Psychology* 18: 65-73.

_____. (1979). *The world technique.* London: George Allen & Unwin.

Neumann, E. (1954). *The origins and history of consciousness.* Princeton: Princeton Univ. Press.

_____. (1973). *The child: Structure and dynamics of the nascent personality.* New York: Harper Colophon.

Noyes, M. (1981). Sandplay imagery: An aid to teaching reading. *Academic Therapy* 17: 231-37.

Reed, J. P. (1975). *Sand magic experience in miniature: A non-verbal therapy for children.* Albuquerque, N.M.: JPR Press.

Stewart, L. H. (1982). Sandplay and Jungian analysis. In *Jungian analysis,* ed. M. Stein, 204-18. La Salle, IL.: Open Court.

Wells, H. G. (1911). *Floor games.* New York: Arno Press.

Valuable Books for Art Educators and Therapists

Rosegarden and Labyrinth   SEONAID M. ROBERTSON

With care and precision and aided by years of experience, Seonaid Robertson explores the relationship between art and psyche. Focusing on the drawings of children and adolescents, she views these first products of the imagination against the background of artistic and cultural history. Illustrations, index. (xxix, 216 pp.)

Color Symbolism

These six papers from the Eranos Yearbook 1972 present a lasting reference work by the most eminent authorities in their fields. Izutsu on Far Eastern art and philosophy; Benz on Christian visions; Rowe on the ancient world; Zahan on African symbolism; Huyghe on Western painting; Portmann on color sense and its meaning in biology. (202 pp.)

Waking Dreams   MARY WATKINS

The riches of daydreams, active imagination, and imaginal others show the relevance of fantasy to the practice of psychotherapy, education, and the drama of individual lives. Historical, critical, and clinical, this book describes European and American approaches to the image, delivering the reader to a close look at his/her own relation to the imaginal world. (viii, 174 pp.)

Broodmales   NOR HALL, WARREN R. DAWSON

In the folk customs of couvade—"brooding" or "hatching"—a man takes on the events of a woman's body—pregnancy, labor, nursing—so that her experience becomes his. Introducing Dawson's 1929 "Custom of Couvade," Hall supplies biographical data about social anthropologists at the turn of the century and then looks inward at the physical ground of the customs they labeled bizarre. Dawson's ethnological classic collects material from accounts of explorers and informants from the 1700s to the 1900s. (173 pp.)

The Cult of Childhood   GEORGE BOAS

Could our fascination with our early years and the issues of child abuse, abortion, family therapy—and even developmental psychology—mean that we are caught in a myth of ideal purity and innocence? Innocence, rather than the true nature of children, may be a fond fantasy about them. By examining the *idea* of childhood, Boas exposes the buried assumptions that continue to influence nearly everything we do and say about children. Concise, intelligent, reliable. (120 pp.)

Fathers and Mothers   BLY, HILLMAN, VITALE ET AL.

Psychology in a different key: through the voice of writers! Twelve chapters that free the reader from the trap of thinking about the family always in the same way. Robert Bly and James Hillman explore and explain how and why fathers and sons must wrestle each other in the agonies of their love. Ursula K. Le Guin reveals woman between Persephone and mother, while Marion Woodman shows how the image of mother can change its shapes and colors during therapy. Others tell of the stepmother, the mothering of desire and what's really the matter with mother. Here, too, are the classic essay by James Hillman on the hero and the mother's son, that of Erich Neumann on matriarchal moon consciousness, and C. G. Jung's original 1938 version of his "The Mother Archetype." (259 pp.)

SPRING PUBLICATIONS, INC • P.O. BOX 222069 • DALLAS, TEXAS 75222